MANAGING
TIME

David Fontana

Personal and Professional Development

SERIES EDITORS:

Glynis M. Breakwell is Professor of Psychology and Head of the Psychology Department at the University of Surrey.

David Fontana is Reader in Educational Psychology at University of Wales College of Cardiff, and Professor Catedrático, University of Minho, Portugal.

Glenys Parry is Director of Psychology Services for Sheffield Health Authority.

The books in this series are designed to help readers use psychological insights, theories and methods to address issues which arise regularly in their own personal and professional lives and which affect how they manage their jobs and careers. Psychologists have a great deal to say about how to improve our work styles. The emphasis in this series is upon presenting psychology in a way which is easily understood and usable. We are committed to enabling our readers to use psychology, applying it for themselves to themselves.

The books adopt a highly practical approach. Readers are confronted with examples and exercises which require them to analyse their own situation and review carefully what they think, feel and do. Such analyses are necessary precursors in coming to an understanding of where and what changes are needed, or can reasonably be made.

These books do not reflect any single approach in psychology. The editors come respectively from social, educational and clinical branches of the discipline. They work together with the authors to ensure that each book provides a fair and comprehensive review of the psychology relevant to the issues discussed.

Each book deals with a clearly defined target and can stand alone. But combined they form an integrated and broad resource, making wide areas of psychological expertise more freely accessible.

OTHER TITLES IN THE SERIES

Interpersonal Conflicts at Work by Robert J. Edelmann

Personal and Professional Development

MANAGING TIME

David Fontana

Reader in Educational Psychology
University of Wales College of Cardiff
and
Professor Catedrático
University of Minho, Portugal

BPS
BOOKS Published by The British Psychological Society

First published in 1993 by BPS Books (The British Psychological Society),
St Andrews House, 48 Princess Road East, Leicester LE1 7DR.

A catalogue record for this book is available from the British Library.

ISBN 1 85433 089 6 paperback
ISBN 1 85433 088 8 hardback

Typeset by Litho Link Limited, Welshpool, Powys, Wales
Printed in Great Britain by BPCC Wheatons Ltd, Exeter

Contents

For Lucilia . . .
who always wants to manage time

INTRODUCTION

This book is based on the premise that good time-management can be learnt. This learning may take longer for some of us than for others, but none of us should find the strategies and procedures involved too daunting in prospect or too difficult in execution. You may wish to read the book straight through first, in order to gain an overall picture of good time-management, and then go back and complete the practical exercises which it contains, or you may prefer to do these exercises as you go along. Either way, you should recognize that the incorporation of a complete programme of good time-management into your professional life is not something that can happen overnight, and it is important to see it as a long-term commitment.

Once you have established a workable programme of good time-management, the benefits will be so obvious in terms of greater productivity and professional fulfilment and in terms of reduced stress and anxiety, that the programme will quickly become self-sustaining. While you are working towards these benefits however, it is important not to become discouraged or to allow yourself to slip back into the old ways. Good time-management demands a degree of commitment and perseverance, and a readiness to stay with (and congratulate yourself on) each advance, no matter how small.

The inspiration for this book comes from a number of sources. These are chiefly published research in psychology and in management, together with my own experience over the years in running stress-management workshops with professional groups, where the effective management of time is usually one of the major themes under consideration. And perhaps I should not entirely forget Lewis Carroll, who, in his full life as lecturer, cleric and writer, saved enough time to relax on the riverbank in the peace of a summer's afternoon.

Chapter One

Time as Finite Capital

There is no better way to begin than by quoting a passage from *Through the Looking-Glass*. It will be familiar to most readers, though I wonder how many of us have ever paused to think about its full implications.

> *Just at this moment, somehow or other, they began to run. . . . the Queen kept crying 'Faster!' but Alice felt she could not go faster, though she had no breath to say so. . . . The most curious part of the thing was, that the trees and the other things round them never changed places at all: however fast they went, they never seemed to pass anything . . . they went so fast that at last they seemed to skim through the air, hardly touching the ground with their feet, till suddenly . . . they stopped.*
>
> *Alice looked round her in great surprise. 'Why, I do believe we've been under this tree all the time! Everything's just as it was!'*
>
> *'Of course it is', said the Queen . . . 'here, you see, it takes all the running you can do, to keep in the same place. If you want to get somewhere else, you must run twice as fast as that!'*

It's easy to smile at Alice's plight. Yet there is something very familiar about it. In fact there are few passages in the whole of literature that represent more clearly the frantic efforts we all make for much of our professional lives simply to keep abreast of time. ' "I wonder if all the things move along with us?", thought poor puzzled Alice', and Alice was right to wonder. For time, like the Looking-Glass world in which Alice found herself, is never still. Time has a habit of moving inexorably from under our feet, hurrying from the present to the past, and demanding, like the Red Queen, that we run faster and faster in a vain effort to make progress against it.

Hot and thirsty from her exertions, Alice then hears the Red Queen say 'I know what *you'd* like', and is given a biscuit which she eats 'as well as she could: and it was *very* dry; and she thought she had never been so nearly choked in all her life. . . . "Thirst quenched, I hope?" said the Queen'. So not only is Alice forced to run at top speed in order to get nowhere at all, but her running earns her the very opposite of what she actually needs. In much the same way, we often find that in spite of our mad efforts to keep up with time, the rewards we receive are directly contrary to the ones we really want.

WHY DOESN'T EFFORT ALWAYS GAIN RESULTS?

Why is this so? Why is it that our efforts at keeping up with time are sometimes so counter-productive? And why are we forced to make such frantic efforts in the first place? Alice was dragged along hand-in-hand by the Red Queen ('and still the Queen cried "Faster! Faster!" and dragged her along'), but in the absence of the Red Queen, who is it who does the dragging? I said a moment ago that it is time itself that demands we keep running, but this is only part of the picture. Certainly it is time that demands we keep moving, but time doesn't dictate to us the form this movement should take. There may be many other, and better, ways of moving than running to such little purpose as Alice.

And indeed there are better ways, as in our more relaxed moments we all realize. For it is we ourselves, or rather our disorganized and inefficient ways of using time, that play the role of the Red Queen in our lives. And as often as not it is we ourselves who ensure that after all our exertions we end up not with a metaphorical glass of water but with a metaphorical dry biscuit.

WHY DO WE BEHAVE IN THIS WAY?

For many people, the answer has something to do with the failure to acknowledge the real nature of time in relation to human life. As a small boy I remember listening to one of those earnest improving children's programmes BBC Radio used to put out, in which the speaker held forth on how we should make best use of time. I remember neither the name of the speaker nor much of what he said, but one of his metaphors stuck in my mind. It was that *time is capital and not renewable income*, capital which we are forced to draw on every moment of our lives, with the result that it is constantly dwindling. What is more, there is no way of replenishing our capital; once it is gone, it is gone forever.

A depressing message you might think. But it meant, I told

myself, that time is something precious. I didn't then (and thankfully still don't) subscribe to the view that time should never be used for loafing about and experiencing the sheer joy of being alive, or that the devil has so little to do that he or she hangs around just waiting to put mischief into idle hands. But I did, thanks to that unknown broadcaster, realize in that moment that we all have responsibility for our own capital. If time is wasted – used in activities that bring no benefit to ourselves or to others – then it is our *own* capital we are wasting. Since the capital belongs to us we have a perfect right to waste it if we wish, but it is no good blaming our wasteful ways upon someone else.

This view of time is indisputable. The minutes of our lives *are* capital rather than renewable income, and when a minute has gone (is *spent*), it is irrecoverable. Science may not yet understand the true nature of time, but for practical purposes it flows from the future to the past, and each of us has a finite number of years in which to experience this flow, and to find more productive ways of using it than Alice's mad dash alongside the Red Queen.

BUT I DO MY BEST

By now you may be protesting that you do appreciate how limited and irreplaceable time is, and that this is the very reason why you find yourself running so hard. Your problem, you may be saying, is not that you ignore the real nature of time but that you recognize it only too well. And you may be adding that the help you need is with organizing your time more effectively, not with recognizing its finite nature. It is our very failure to fully realize the importance of time that lies behind our disorganized use of it. Most of us are 'busy' all the time and 'work hard', but we may never have grasped that unless our busyness and hard work are effective, we are wasting our capital in much the same way (and probably inflicting more damage on our mental and physical health in the process) as if we were sitting doing nothing.

The upshot of this is that any programme designed to help us manage our time efficiently must start with our realization that time is precious, consequently motivating us to use this finite asset with the same care we would devote to the spending of gold coins. No matter how good our planning and intentions, unless we start with this motivation no programme for managing time will be effective for very long. We may start well, but we will end up with the all too frequent experience of making good resolutions, sticking to them enthusiastically for a few days or so, and then inexorably returning to our old bad habits of – to coin a phrase – muddling along at top speed.

Exercise 1 is aimed at helping you reflect further on the importance of the right kind of motivation if you are really to value time as you should. It takes longer than the other exercises in this book, because it is one of the most vital. Without the experiences it brings we cannot fully recognize how fleeting time really is. When people have completed an exercise of this kind they often say things like, 'I thought back to an event in my childhood and it seemed like yesterday'; 'I found myself wondering where all the time has gone'; 'It seemed as if the years have passed by like a dream'. People also often say how much more quickly time seems to go by as they grow older, and how much more they come to regret the time they feel they have wasted. But they can take heart. Once the motivation to manage time is established, and once there is a proper sense of urgency about it, the ways of managing it can be acquired, both in terms of one's relationship to oneself and in one's relationship to others. And although managing time may at first sight seem to involve you in yet more work (organizing yourself, planning programmes, developing systems), the benefits are clear and impressive. Let me list some of them:

- increased effectiveness and efficiency;
- higher productivity;
- increased leisure time (working more effectively means you have more time for yourself);
- enhanced job satisfaction (we all enjoy work more if we are on top of it instead of it on top of us);
- reduced stress (managing time effectively takes much of the pressure off us);
- more opportunity to switch off after hours (completing more of our work-load during the day makes it easier for our minds to relax at night);
- more room for forward planning and for long-term solutions (if we aren't struggling just to keep up with ourselves we have space in which to look ahead);
- higher creativity (creativity flourishes best if we can free time to sit, think and daydream a little).

VALUING TIME

EXERCISE 1

It is one thing to recognize the importance of time at the theoretical level, quite another to do so at the practical and emotional levels. And in our relationship to time, as in so many other things, it is by engaging our feelings that we are best able to appreciate the value time has in our lives.

In order to undertake this exercise properly, it is best to choose a time and place where you are unlikely to be disturbed. Unplug the telephone and sit in a comfortable position in an upright chair. Now concentrate your attention upon your breathing. As you do so, become aware that each breath takes place *within time*. Each breath occupies moments of your life, of your finite capital. Be aware of time flowing with your in-breaths and out-breaths. Keep your mind peaceful and relaxed. The purpose of this exercise isn't to make you feel panicky about the passing of time, but to bring to mind the importance of each moment, and help you savour it as an experience rather in the way that you savour a piece of music or a work of art.

Now let your mind drift to a moment in the past. It can be a recent event or one from long ago – the important thing is that it should be something that carries clear, and preferably pleasant memories. Allow your mind to dwell on the event, recapturing as many of the details as possible. When you have done this, let your mind come forward across the intervening gap of time. As you do so, note some of the significant events which took place during it. Note them as if you were scanning a picture panorama and pausing briefly on certain images that stand out.

Be aware in this scanning process that the mind is travelling along a road of memories from the past to the present. Each of the images you see existed once in real time, but now exists only in your memory. The people, the things, the events they represent are no longer present in direct experience. They belong only to the past.

Take as long as you like over this exercise, but don't become lost in thought over any individual event. You are exploring time, not memories themselves. Allow feelings to arise in response to the exercise (nostalgia, pleasure, regret, gratitude), but don't become caught up in any of them. Make them part of the scanning process, so that as you scan each event and pass on, so you scan the feelings associated with it and pass on. Don't become involved in judging whether the events or the feelings indicate that you made good or bad use of time. This is not what the exercise is for. Concentrate instead on the recognition that all these events happened in moments which were once in the present but which are now lost forever.

Finish the exercise by bringing your attention back to your breathing, and recognizing that the present moment is all that you have. Even the exercise on which you've just been engaged now exists only as a memory. Everything follows the law of time which decrees that all we have in our lives is *now*, the present moment. *Now* is when you are spending your precious capital, so *now* is always the moment that must be put to use if you really want to manage time.

Let me also list some of the things that good time-management most definitely is not. It isn't:

- so-called Type A behaviour, that is, restlessly and demandingly driving oneself and everyone else to the limit; good time management involves pacing oneself sensibly and finding time for leisure pursuits;
- a ruthless and selfish approach to life; good time-management frees one to be potentially more aware of and sensitive towards others, and to have more time for them;
- efficiency gone mad; good time-managers are just as human as anyone else – the difference is that they know life works best if organized properly;
- inflexible or uncreative; good time-management allows one the space to adapt and modify as the need arises, and to have more time to incubate and express creative ideas.

PERSONAL FULFILMENT

These and other aspects of time-management will, I hope, become clearer as we go through the book. But let me conclude this chapter by referring to what is perhaps the most potent benefit of good time-management, namely enhanced personal fulfilment and self-regard. We are much better able to fulfil our potential in life, and to think well of ourselves, if we are conscious that we get things done rather than behave ineffectually. Eric Erikson, in his well-known model of the development of personality throughout life (Erikson, 1968) sees *generativity* (achievement, usefulness, creativity) as the most important life-goal of mature adulthood. Unless we are able to attain this goal, he argues, for most of us there will be inevitable feelings of stagnation and of failure. We will see ourselves as unable to reach our potential, unable to act as significant members of the community, and unable to make a genuine contribution to life.

If we succeed in finding the fulfilment that generativity brings, we are also better able, in due course, to experience the *self-acceptance* that Erikson sees as the goal of later life. This form of mature self-acceptance comes from the ability to look back on a life in which we made proper use of whatever abilities and talents we were fortunate enough to possess. It comes through freedom from the persistent wish to put back the clock, and an absence of the nagging recognition that if we had our time over again we would make better use of it, waste it less often, and be more conscious of its transitory nature.

Recognizing the importance of these goals adds further to our motivation to manage time effectively. Once armed with this motivation, we can begin to look at the attitudes of mind which lie behind effective management.

Chapter Two

Developing the Right Attitude of Mind

Once we have a clear, unequivocal commitment to managing time effectively, the next step is to develop the attitude of mind that goes with it. On the face of it, this seems easy enough. But my own experience from running stress-management workshops shows that, next to insufficient motivation, the failure to develop the correct attitude of mind is the major reason why many people, even though familiar with some of the necessary time-management techniques, fail to practise them with any consistency. The following case study illustrates this.

❏ *Morgan: a case study of the wrong attitude*
Morgan is an account executive for an advertising agency and has worked in advertising for five years, after graduating with a good university degree. He is personable, likeable and enthusiastic, and by his own admission is good at his job. However, he admits to mounting anxiety over what he calls his 'chronically disorganized lifestyle':

'I must be the world's worst. People are always telling me I'm earmarked for big things in the advertising world, and this scares me. I'm ambitious and I want to get on, but the job is already eating up my life. I work harder than anyone else in the agency: I get there earlier in the mornings, I stay later at night, I'm forever taking work home with me, and I've a feeling my health is beginning to suffer. Being promoted and taking on even more responsibility will mean that things can only get worse. But if I turn down promotion I know I'm going to hate myelf. I keep trying to organize my time more effectively, but I can't keep it up. I just don't have that kind of mind.'

There is no doubting Morgan's intelligence, or his motivation to change his disorganized way of doing things. He recognizes the problems that his present working habits are causing him, and is anxious about the even greater problems they are likely to cause in the future. Since he claims to 'keep trying to organize' his time more effectively, he appears to have some knowledge of the strategies he needs to employ, but he excuses his failure to put them to proper use by the claim that he just doesn't 'have that kind of mind'.

The first step in convincing Morgan that this excuse was groundless was to ask him what 'kind of mind' is needed to manage time effectively. This question is best tackled in the form of the short exercise which follows.

THE QUALITIES OF A GOOD TIME-MANAGER

EXERCISE 2

Imagine for a moment that you are the most effective time-manager in a highly efficient office. Your colleagues all admire you and take you as their role model. One day, out of interest, they decide to list the qualities which make you the way you are. What qualities would this list contain? In other words, what qualities would you have to possess in order to be recognized as the most effective time-manager around?

In response to *Exercise 2*, Morgan wrote down without much hesitation:

- *clarity of thinking*
- *decisiveness*
- *single-mindedness*
- *good memory*
- *determination*
- *a methodical approach*
- *punctuality*
- *calmness*
- *objectivity*
- *rationality*
- *leadership*

The chances are that your own list is similar to Morgan's. Now go through your list and underline all those qualities which in your professional life you have *never* been able to show. When Morgan tried to do so, he found he couldn't underline any of them, and admitted that at some time or other he'd shown them all.

WHAT 'KIND OF MIND' IS NECESSARY TO MANAGE TIME?

For Morgan and for the rest of us, *Exercise 2* is a simple way of demonstrating that we all have 'the kind of mind' necessary to manage time. We all have the power to think clearly, to show decisiveness, to be single-minded and so on; the main reason we fail to show these qualities more consistently is that they require a certain amount of effort. We tend to think that, through an accident of nature, they come easily to those lucky people who do have 'that kind of mind', and are difficult for the rest of us. But this isn't the case. More often it is a matter of developing what is already there, through effort followed by the right kind of learning. Our understanding of the psychology of learning (to say nothing of simple common sense) tells us that those behaviours which produce desirable results are likely to be repeated (Skinner, 1972). Thus once we make a consistent and sustained effort to manage time more effectively, we soon begin to find that it starts to bring benefits, and this in turn makes us more likely to repeat these behaviours, which leads to more benefits, which leads to the use of more time-effective behaviours and so on. In other words, we *learn* to be effective by virtue of the improved results which our efforts actually bring.

THE IMPORTANCE OF CLEAR OBJECTIVES

If we return to the case of Morgan we find that he claimed he did 'keep trying to organize' his time more effectively. So why didn't his efforts lead to the kind of upward learning spiral I've just described? If his efforts produced good results, then surely he should have 'learnt' to become a more efficient time-manager? So why didn't he? There could be several answers. Firstly, he may have been using the wrong strategies. Secondly, he may have been using the right strategies but not applying them consistently enough. And thirdly, he might not have been properly aware of the improved results that these strategies were bringing him.

The first two possibilities are covered later when we come to discuss actual time-management strategies and their use, but the third of them concerns us now. When asked as a follow-up to *Exercise 2* to list the benefits that his attempts to organize his time more effectively brought him, Morgan was vague and uncertain, and sheltered behind generalities like 'I seemed to get more done' and 'I felt less tired when I got home'. It was clear that none of his attempts had been aimed at the attainment of specific time-management goals. In other words he hadn't tried to manage *this* aspect of his time in order to achieve *that* definite result. There was no evidence that his efforts at time-management had ever been carried out with clear objectives in mind. This showed that although he wanted to be more effective, he wasn't even clear what 'effectiveness' meant in terms of actual goals to be achieved.

In consequence, Morgan had failed to learn from his efforts. They probably did bring him some positive results, but since he wasn't able to recognize in detail what these results were, he wasn't really experiencing them as tangible rewards. His whole approach was vague and diffuse, and it was hardly surprising that on his own admission he was unable to keep up his good intentions for any length of time. They were sporadic, haphazard, and ultimately unproductive. And meanwhile he went on confusing hard work with effective work, driving himself into the ground in the process (we're back to Alice and the Red Queen again) and well on the way to damaging his health as a consequence. Incidentally, his reference to health raises the crucial point that managing time effectively ultimately means managing ourselves effectively; that is, managing our physical and psychological resources in a way that enables us to pace ourselves properly and remain able to function efficiently. Driving ourselves into the ground is ultimately of no use to anyone, least of all to ourselves.

Morgan still had to learn that good time-managers are people who are able not only to meet all reasonable demands upon their time, but are able to do so without draining away too much of their physical and psychological resources. They realize that getting things done is by itself not good enough, we have to be able to get things done *economically*. Thus, good time-management has a dual function in that it allows us to:

• operate effectively in life

and

• protect ourselves from that great enemy of professional life, psychological and/or physical burn-out.

Activities which don't serve both these functions do not come under the heading of good time-management, and are unlikely to sustain for any length of time the generativity which I earlier referred to as a goal of mature adulthood.

DOES TEMPERAMENT PLAY A PART?

Once he recognized how difficult it was for him to list the specific benefits of his time-management efforts, Morgan was able to accept how disorganized these attempts had been. He was even able to admit that perhaps he had been too ready to offer the excuse that he didn't have the 'kind of mind' necessary to manage time. But he still wondered if some people were by temperament better able to learn the lessons of good time-management than others. Were good time-managers 'born' as well as 'made'?

NATURE VERSUS NURTURE

The relative contributions of nature versus nurture to human behaviour is a perennial question in psychology, and crops up whenever human abilities are being discussed. Do we inherit our personal qualities or do we acquire them through experience? The evidence suggests that certain psychological factors such as our sociability (social extroversion) and our susceptibility to anxiety are influenced by heredity, and the same may be true for other qualities such as adaptability, self-will and the strength of our emotional reactions (for example Horowitz, 1987). Our potential for certain kinds of learning and problem-solving and for certain kinds of creative expression may be influenced in the same way. But in none of these areas is it heredity alone that decides matters. Rather it is the interaction between inherited potential and the environment, between our genes and our learning experiences, that makes us the people we are.

Thus, although it is possible that certain of the qualities identified by Morgan as apparent in good time-managers owe something to heredity, there is little doubt that it is the right kind of learning experiences that determine whether or not they are properly developed. And there is equally little doubt that many of us are offered few of these experiences in our formal education. As children we were constantly admonished by our teachers not to waste time, but most school timetables contained (and still contain) little guidance on how this is best done. The tuition in study habits and higher order learning skills – in short in *learning how to learn* –

that would have initiated us into good time-management skills was conspicuously lacking throughout the education of most of us.

The result is that most of us have little awareness of the real benefits that such skills can bring. And even those benefits which we do achieve often become lost in the confusion which spills over from our inability to manage time in other areas of our lives. Like Morgan, the easiest response is to put all this down to the fact that we just don't 'have the mind for it'. We shift the blame to our heredity, to something over which we have no control, rather than accept that the remedies lie within our own hands. In effect, we *disempower* ourselves rather than *empower* ourselves. And the sustained, systematic determination to acquire and apply the skills necessary to empower ourselves is the essential quality of the good time-manager, a quality that lies potentially within us all.

Therefore, instead of allowing ourselves to retreat into feelings of helplessness when dealing with time, we must accept that we do have the power to handle it effectively and positively, and that if we fail to do so the fault ultimately lies within ourselves rather than within our genes. *Exercise 2* was a way of helping us towards this acceptance. It allowed us to list the personal qualities apparent in good time-managers, and then to challenge ourselves to say that we have none of them. The fact that we have shown even a few of them at some point in our lives indicates that we possess them and that they are ripe for development and use.

This brings me to what is in a sense the overriding message of this chapter. The more we tell ourselves that we don't have 'the kind of mind' necessary to manage time, the more we condition ourselves into believing that we haven't. The evidence from sports psychology and from certain areas of occupational, clinical and educational psychology (Fontana, 1988) is that the ability to think positively about our abilities has a profound effect upon our performance. Giving ourselves messages that have to do with success rather than failure seems in fact to be an essential ingredient in the achievement of full potential. Without such messages, the mind becomes programmed to ideas of failure, low standards, and defeat. The messages we give ourselves are rather like having a teacher or a parent standing at our shoulder, either encouraging us to believe in ourselves and use our abilities, or belittling our every effort and emphasizing over and over again the idea that we are going to fail, rather than the idea that we will succeed. Which approach would be more likely to bring out the best in you?

THE POWER OF POSITIVE THINKING

The phrase 'As you think, so you are' isn't an invention of modern cognitive psychology. It has been found in one form or another in writings going back to the ancient Egyptians. It means quite simply that the way in which we think about ourselves profoundly influences the way we behave. We are, in terms of our self-esteem and our self-identity, largely the creation of our own thinking. In terms of time-management, this means that if we constantly dwell on our own shortcomings, and continually tell ourselves how ineffectual we are and how unlikely we are to get any better, then that is how we will doubtless remain. If, on the other hand, we give ourselves the positive message that we can and will improve, then this positive mental set puts us in a much better position to achieve success. In addition to the points covered in the text, you can help yourself to think positively about your ability to manage time if you:

- Note your successes rather than only your failures; however small these successes may be, congratulate yourself each time they occur, and write them down so that you have a concrete record of them.

- Give yourself (in addition to the more major objectives discussed in due course in Chapter 4) a few small realistic time-management targets each day (for example, 10 minutes for coffee instead of 15, no phone call to last beyond a set period of time, no social chatting in the corridors) and add each success to your record.

- Catch yourself each time you make a negative comment about your time-management, and change it into a comment about how you intend to improve (for example, change 'I've wasted so much time this morning' to 'Tomorrow morning I'll save time by not . . .').

- Replace regret for opportunities lost through time-wasting in the past ('If only . . .') with concrete resolutions not to let it happen again ('Next time . . .').

Negative thinking can become a destructive habit. Watch your thoughts more closely, and aim to turn your negative self-attitude around. Don't be unrealistic about this: make positive statements about your time-management abilities which can be translated into actual behaviour. Take short steps. And congratulate yourself on effort as well as on results.

Since all those with the qualities necessary to enter professional life are likely to have the ability to manage time effectively, the essential requirement is to believe in this ability, and to take personal responsibility for making good use of it. In the following chapters I shall discuss some of the techniques which add up to this good use, but we can anticipate them for a moment in order to conclude this chapter with the following equation:

right motivation + right frame of mind + right techniques
= good time-management

Put like that, it doesn't seem so difficult.

Chapter Three

Your Current Use of Time

One of the most valuable gifts one person can give to another is the gift of time. Most of us can, if we're lucky, remember someone – perhaps a teacher or relative – from our younger days who stood out from other adults because they always seemed to have time for us. They were prepared to listen, to guide, to help, when others couldn't be bothered with us or told us briskly to come back later. And most of us acknowledge that one of the hallmarks of good parents is that they make the effort to have time for their children.

It's tempting to imagine that people who can give their time to others in this way are people who have time on their hands, and that we would all be like that if we weren't so rushed off our feet. But the old adage, 'If you want something done, ask a busy person,' isn't far from the truth. People who *have* time are rarely people who have time on their hands. For the most part they are people who value time and what can be done with it, and who have learnt how to make proper use of it in most situations. They are another example of the good time-managers who form the subject of this book. They can't *make* time but they can *find* time, for the simple reason that they try never really to lose it in the first place.

THE FIRST STEPS TOWARDS EFFECTIVE TIME-MANAGEMENT

Having identified in the last chapter that the purpose of good time-management is to allow one to operate effectively in life without dissipating unnecessary energy, and having previously discussed the prior importance of right motivation and of the right frame of mind, we can begin to look at time-management strategies themselves. Obviously, many such strategies are situation-specific, and what is needed in one professional context may be rather different from what is needed in another. Nevertheless, the basic principles of good time-management remain constant right across circumstances, and it is on the strength of these principles that each of us is able to work out the specifics which apply to our own particular case.

If we want to improve on the way in which we use time, we must first of all identify how we are misusing it at present. This is simple common sense. If I want to travel to London, I first have to know where my starting point is. It's no good looking up train or bus timetables to London or to anywhere else if I don't know where I am now. So the first step is to make a detailed survey of how you are currently using (and losing) time. *Exercise 3* (p18) is one way of doing this.

IDENTIFYING YOUR USE OF TIME

What does *Exercise 3* demonstrate to you? Where does most of your time actually go? Of course much of this time isn't wasted, and it is sometimes difficult to draw precise lines between *essential* time (time necessarily spent due to the demands of the job) and *peripheral* time (time which is not actively wasted but which is spent on tasks, such as 'Hunting', often rendered necessary by our own inefficiency. But progress in good time-management demands that we arrive at approximations, and the more closely we study where our time goes, the more accurate these approximations are likely to be. So the follow-up to *Exercise 3* is to identify for each of the categories on your Time Record (excluding Task Time, which we'll return to later) what appears to be *essential* time, *peripheral* time, and *non-essential* time (time clearly wasted). Now carry out the exercise for a second week, noting in more detail what actually happens during peripheral time and non-essential time.

If you have identified that much of the time you spend on the telephone is non-essential, note whether each call is incoming or outgoing, who it was from or who it was to, what the subject of the call was and your estimate of how much of the time spent talking was actually productive. Do the same for meetings and conversations if you suspect that they also contain much non-essential time. With the former, note down the purpose of the meeting, whether your attendance was voluntary or mandatory, and your estimate of how much time appeared to be taken up unnecessarily. With the latter, note down who the conversation was with, whether it was

RECORDING YOUR CURRENT USE OF TIME

EXERCISE 3

For much of the working day many of us are unaware of how quickly the time goes by. We glance at our watches, groan 'that can't *possibly* be the time', and when the day is over complain that we don't know where on earth it actually went. This can happen irrespective of whether or not we happen to enjoy what we are doing.

Most of us don't have a 'typical' working day, so it's of limited use to lay down rigidly the best way of charting our current use of time. But we need to have some idea of how this time is portioned out between the various activities in which we are most frequently involved. This is best done by keeping a record over a whole week. Choose a week which is reasonably representative of your usual working routine, and at the end of each day enter as accurately as you can under relevant headings the time spent on each of the activities concerned. In order to help you with this, try to make scribbled notes during the day of the exact time you switch from one activity to another. At the end of the week, average out your findings so that you get a fair idea of where each day actually goes. Using broad categories, Mintzberg (1973) found, for example, that managers typically spend 22 per cent of their time on desk work (correspondence, proof-reading, paperwork, and so on), 6 per cent on the telephone, 59 per cent in scheduled meetings, 10 per cent in unscheduled meetings, and the rest in miscellaneous activities.

You may want to use the following example as a starting point for your own time record:

continued

continued

TIME RECORD

TIME SPENT EACH DAY
(Hours/Minutes)

ACTIVITY	M	T	W	Th	F
Travel during working hours (trips to see clients, to attend meetings off the premises, etc.)					
Dealing with correspondence					
Telephone (connected with work)					
Telephone (not connected with work)					
Tea/coffee breaks					
Lunch					
Formal Meetings					
Conversations (connected with work)					
Conversations (not connected with work)					
Filing and Record Keeping					
Moving Around the Building (in a large building significant time is spent simply getting from one place to another)					
Writing Up (case notes, reports, etc.)					
Paperwork (form-filling etc.)					
Hunting (time spent searching for documents, letters, etc.)					
Daydreaming					
Task Time (time spent directly on main professional tasks)					

Add any other categories relevant to you (for example, photo-copying, standing-in for colleagues, supervising or training others) which do not appear on the above list (see, for example, Christie 1984, Pearn and Kandola 1988).

initiated by them or by you, and whether it came in the form of an interruption to your other work or not. You can't hope for accuracy but an approximation is quite sufficient. (If all this sounds too demanding, let me reassure you that in one form or another it is a technique frequently used when research is conducted into how professionals use their time).

If you feel you're losing a significant amount of peripheral time in travelling, note down what each journey was for and where it took you. If peripheral time is lost filing (whether computer-aided or not) note down what was being filed and where. If peripheral or non-essential time is lost over lunch or teabreaks, note whether this was because of your own tendency to sit too long over these activities or whether it was due to other people detaining you, for whatever reason. If time is lost hunting for things, note what you were hunting for, why you were hunting for it, where eventually it was found, and why it was mislaid in the first place. If it's lost in daydreaming, note as far as possible the times of day when your daydreaming is most likely to take place (for example, before actually getting down to work on arrival in the morning, the half hour after lunch, mid-afternoon) and the kind of things that tend to set off your daydreams (for example, the prospect of making a start on an activity you dislike or dealing with the morning's correspondence).

In carrying out this follow-up to *Exercise 3*, it is important that you are as specific as possible about the activities involved. The purpose of this is to help you gain a clear picture of how and to what extent precious minutes are allowed to ebb away unproductively each day. Don't take into account whether the time lost was wasted pleasantly or not. Many of the most time-wasting conversations can be the most enjoyable ones. The colleagues or clients who are most responsible for taking up your time unnecessarily may be the people you like best. The meetings at which most time is frittered away may be the very ones in which you take most interest and in which you do much of the talking. Simply note all these things down, objectively and non-judgementally, without allowing your feelings or likes and dislikes to enter into it.

Let's look at the example of how Brian, an administrative assistant in local government, logged details for a single day in just one of the categories that concerned him most, namely 'Hunting'. This is an easy category to look at, since Brian regarded the time it consumed as all peripheral (and thus avoidable).

❏ *Brian: a case study in time loss*

Hunting

Object Lost	Why Needed	Where Found	Why Lost
letter	urgent reply required	top of filing cabinet	put down randomly when phone rang
(Time Lost: 6 minutes)			
glasses	reading	gents' toilet	removed to wash face
(Time Lost: 4 minutes)			
pen	signing letters	under in-tray	in-tray in wrong place
(Time Lost: 3 minutes)			
report	attendance at meeting	not found	thrown away in error?
(Time Lost: 20 minutes)			
coffee cup	morning coffee	colleague's room	dishonest colleague!
(Time Lost: 2 minutes)			
memo	check details	briefcase	forgot I'd taken it home
(Time Lost: 5 minutes)			
phone number	call required	on desk	scribbled on piece of paper
(Time Lost: 3 minutes)			
aide memoir	figures needed	filing cabinet	misfiled
(Time Lost: 2 minutes)			

Brian was surprised by the fact that in one working day he'd lost 45 minutes hunting for things. The lost report had been the single major culprit, and had caused him most anxiety, but even discounting this he'd lost 25 minutes looking for things which need not have been mislaid in the first place. It was easy to see from the list that a small amount of organization could have avoided most, if not all, of this expenditure of peripheral time, as we shall see when organization is discussed in Chapter 4. Mercifully Brian didn't lose this amount of time every day, but averaged out over the week he still found that he lost around 20 minutes a day, often looking for something which had been filed safely enough, but under the wrong heading, or put in a 'safe place' which eluded his memory.

DECISION TIME

There's no doubting the desirability, in theory, of saving as much peripheral and non-essential time as possible. One estimate (Christie, 1984) suggests on the basis of previous research that as much as 20 per cent (that is, one day a week) of office principals' time is lost in activities which come under these headings. But in practice matters aren't quite as straightforward as they seem. For saving this time often means that we have to change some, and perhaps many, working habits that are much less obviously undesirable than hunting for lost objects. This may involve quite major changes in our behaviour, particularly in the way in which we relate to others, and, not unnaturally, we may be reluctant to make these changes. I pointed out that it was important to carry out the follow-up to *Exercise 3* without taking into account whether the time lost was wasted pleasantly or not. But now that you are faced with your completed Time Record chart, it is inevitable that you will start making judgements, and that you may find that it is the very things that make work most enjoyable that waste the most time.

This isn't to suggest that you are deliberately wasting this time. It's simply to acknowledge that the moments of socializing with colleagues, of chatting on the telephone, of sitting an extra few minutes over a cup of coffee or over lunch, or of engaging in the challenge of protracted debate during meetings, can be what humanize our work for us. And there's another danger. We may be afraid that if we reduce the time spent in this way not only will we find work less fun, but we will also distance ourselves from colleagues. In any context it can be difficult to change our social behaviours because these behaviours are embedded in the social lives of others, and colleagues and friends may see such changes as unwelcome to them personally. In addition, the increased efficiency that may result from our changed behaviours may be seen by colleagues as a challenge to their own working practices, and may be resented or resisted by them accordingly.

THE COST OF TIME-MANAGEMENT

Thus, although managing time brings great benefits to us, it can also exact a price, not only in terms of the initial effort and determination we have to put into it, but in terms of the sacrifice we may have to make of valued aspects of the *status quo*. It would be easy to say that we can reduce this price by only changing those time-wasting aspects that we actively dislike, but this is rarely good enough. The things we dislike may be the very things that we can't change (for example, there may be meetings which we have to attend, however much we dislike them, frustrating time-consuming journeys and visits that we have to make). And human nature being what it is, we may already have found ways of avoiding at least some of the more unwelcome aspects of our working lives.

If we *really* want to manage time, we have to be disciplined enough to eliminate some of the things that are highly enjoyable in themselves, and disciplined enough to persevere even in the face of any consequent resistance that comes from colleagues and friends. We have to commit ourselves to change, however uncomfortable it may at first seem to be both for ourselves and for others. Anne is an example of the need for this commitment.

❑ *Anne: a case study in the need for commitment*
Anne is a middle manager in a retailing company. Married and with two school-age children, she found that her life was becoming increasingly hectic and that her poor time-management was making it very difficult for her to cope. But the problem with Anne was that no matter how vehemently she protested that she wanted to be a good time-manager, and no matter how many time-management strategies she tried, she showed no signs of improvement. This was strange, particularly as Anne is an intelligent and able person, and the strategies concerned were well-suited to her situation. She would try each strategy for a short time, then protest it didn't work, usually advancing a curiously lame explanation. Gradually the lameness of these explanations helped to make Anne's problem clear. When she protested she wanted to be a good time-manager, what she really meant was that she wanted the results of good time-management while continuing with her existing life-style and working practices.

It was only when Anne realized that this was not possible that she stood much chance of improvement. The way forward then became clear. Since she found it hard to change her life-style, the solution was to arrange her new time-management strategies into the form of a hierarchy, so that she could tackle the least disruptive ones first. As she came to reap the benefits of these, so her determination to graduate to the more far-reaching ones become stronger.

The comforting thing for Anne, as for the rest of us, is that as the benefits of good time-management become more apparent and the rewards begin to accumulate, so it becomes progressively easier to do without the extra time spent chatting in the corridor or the extra minutes spent sitting over a mid-morning break. And once this happens, and we become more aware of the price we have been paying for ineffectual time-management, it can be actively frustrating to be trapped into a long conversation about irrelevant matters while precious minutes of life tick away.

TIME-MANAGEMENT ON-TASK

We now need to go back to our Time Record and look at the entries under 'Task-Time'. These represent time spent directly on our main professional tasks, in other words *essential* time. However, simply because this is essential time we mustn't assume it is necessarily *effective* time. We may think we are working product-ively, whereas in fact if we were to reorganize our working practices we would almost invariably find that we could get very much more done in the same space of time. We tend to be creatures of habit, and become attached to (or entrenched in) our existing ways of doing things. It becomes an effort to change, and an effort to maintain the new habits once change has taken place. We like the familiar, the known. And we can so easily justify this liking by arguing that new ways of doing things are all right in theory but won't work in practice, or that it will take so long to explain them to those working with us that in the long run we won't be saving time at all.

In the end, such justifications are forms of self-deception. Let's test matters by looking closely at what happens under 'Task Time'. *Exercise 4* (p26) enables you to look at where the time listed under this category actually goes. If you are a lecturer, how much time do you actually spend lecturing? If you are a researcher, how much time is spent researching? If you are a clinician or a social worker, how much time is actually spent with clients? If you are a manager, how much time is actually spent in managing or in overseeing production in those areas for which you carry management responsibility?

When carrying out *Exercise 4*, some people, particularly those whose jobs are mainly administrative, say that much of their task time is spent writing letters, talking on the telephone, form-filling, attending meetings, and reading and writing reports. This is fine, and in their case all their time has perhaps been listed under these categories, leaving them nothing to enter under 'Task Time'. But even for many administrators *Exercise 4* can show that much of the day is actually spent doing things which really lie outside their terms of employment. A common complaint is: 'I'm paid as an administrator/manager/head teacher, yet I spend most of my life doing the work of an office junior/messenger/secretary'.

It isn't necessary to strive for strict accuracy over the minor details of *Exercise 4*. Its purpose is to help you identify where your current on-task working habits are losing time for you, and what these current on-task working habits actually *are*. Until we find the space to sit down and take a hard look at them, many of these habits will have become so routine that for the most part we're no longer fully conscious of them.

The 60 questions in *Exercise 4* are concerned with some of the most frequent causes of time lost in professional life. There is some overlap between the three areas into which they are grouped. However, these areas provide us with a useful way of dividing up our examination of good time-management, and they will be used in the chapters that follow. Many of the questions are self-explanatory, in that the issues they prompt you to think about are clear and nothing further needs to be said about them. Other questions raise more complex matters, and these will be dealt with at appropriate points as we go through the book.

In the first area, *You and your tasks*, a 'Yes' response to questions, 2, 3, 5, 6, 8, 9, 10, 11, and 20 and a 'No' response to the remainder suggests problems with time-management. In the second area, *You and yourself*, a 'Yes' response to questions 21, 24, 28, 29, 30, 32, 34, 35, 36, 39, 40, 41, 44, and 45 and a 'No' response to the remainder carries a similar suggestion. In the case of area three, *You and others*, time-management problems are suggested by answering 'Yes' to questions 49, 50, 52, 53, 54 and 55, and 'No' to the remainder.

Before moving on, however, what have you learnt from your responses to *Exercise 4*? These responses provide you with a profile of your personal approach to time on-task. In studying them, can you see any patterns emerging? For example, do you seem reasonably able to manage time in relation to one of the three areas

USE OF TASK TIME

EXERCISE 4

This exercise helps you to look at some issues relevant to your time on-task. Since the nature of time on-task varies from one job to another, the exercise provides you with a set of general questions designed to help you reflect upon your own particular situation. Don't ponder too long over any particular question. Concentrate upon establishing the general pattern of your approach to time on-task, nothing more. The exercise isn't intended to yield an efficiency score of any kind, so don't regard yourself as being on trial.

You and your tasks

1. Do you keep any kind of time-planner for each week showing how you are going to allocate your time during the days ahead?   Yes/No
2. Do you often have feelings of panic when you think of how much you have to do?   Yes/No
3. Do you frequently find yourself trying to attend to several jobs at the same time?   Yes/No
4. When you set out on a task, do you have clear objectives as to what you want to achieve?   Yes/No
5. Are you constantly struggling with a long backlog of work waiting to be done?   Yes/No
6. When you've been out of your office for a while, do you frequently return to find a list of telephone callers who want you to ring them back?   Yes/No
7. Do you have time to plan ahead, or are you frequently overtaken by events?   Yes/No
8. Do you often have to stay late in order to finish work? Yes/No
9. Do you regularly have to take routine work home with you in order to complete it?   Yes/No
10. When you've been away on duties connected with your work, is your desk piled high on your return?   Yes/No
11. Are you constantly rushing to meet deadlines?   Yes/No
12. Do you review your activities at reasonable intervals, in order to monitor your performance and discard unnecessary duties?   Yes/No
13. Do you know where to look up (or ask for) the information you are likely to need in your job?   Yes/No
14. Have you procedures for keeping necessary records (as opposed to relying mainly on your memory)?   Yes/No
15. Have you strategies for helping you remember the things that have to be kept in mind?   Yes/No
16. Do you keep notes of meetings, and file them methodically?   Yes/No

continued

continued ▬▬ ▬ ▬ ▬ ▬ ▬ ▬ ▬ ▬ ▬ ▬ ▬ ▬ ▬ ▬ ▬

17. Are you clear as to the priorities in your job?　　　　Yes/No
18. Can you find routine things like files, telephone
numbers, lists and addresses as soon as you want them?　　Yes/No
19. Do you group tasks together, so that your mind isn't forced
frequently to switch from one kind of job to another?　　Yes/No
20. Do you sometimes wake up at night remembering
things you should have done during the day?　　Yes/No

You and yourself

21. Do you frequently find yourself putting off jobs
until 'later'?　　Yes/No
22. Do you usually *start* the working day in a positive
mood?　　Yes/No
23. Do you usually *finish* the working day in a positive
mood?　　Yes/No
24. Are you easily distracted from the task in hand?　　Yes/No
25. Can you remember, in reasonable detail, how you
spent your working day yesterday?　　Yes/No
26. Are you aware of the time (during the day, week
or month) when you are likely to be at your best for
tackling particular tasks?　　Yes/No
27. Would you (and your colleagues) describe you as
a punctual person?　　Yes/No
28. Are you aware of any particular habits or
idiosyncracies in your working style which you recognize
objectively as counterproductive? (If so, list them.)　　Yes/No
29. Do you frequently feel over-tired when at work?　　Yes/No
30. Do you often have difficulty in getting started on a
new task or on the day's work?　　Yes/No
31. Are you able to turn your mind back quickly to your
work after interruptions?　　Yes/No
32. Do you frequently take on tasks at too short notice?　　Yes/No
33. Are you determined to finish a task whenever
possible once you have taken it on?　　Yes/No
34. Are you constantly making lists on scraps of paper
of things awaiting your attention?　　Yes/No
35. Do you sometimes find notes or names or
numbers in your own handwriting without remembering
what they are about?　　Yes/No
36. Do you sometimes find yourself trying to recall
that 'brilliant' idea you had recently but which has gone
clean out of your mind?　　Yes/No
37. Are you confident that you avoid creating
unnecessary work for yourself?　　Yes/No
38. Can you relax when you have free time in the
office or at home, or is your mind constantly
returning to your work?　　Yes/No

continued

continued

39. Are you rather slow in making decisions? Yes/No
40. Do you pride yourself on always being busy? Yes/No
41. Do you spend time on minor details, in spite of the fact that many tasks obey the law of diminishing returns? Yes/No
42. Are you able to identify the principles underlying tasks and information, rather than frequently becoming lost in the minor details? Yes/No
43. Can you recognize those times when a short break will improve the efficiency with which you're working, and act accordingly? Yes/No
44. Do you often 'forget' to tackle unpleasant tasks at the right time? Yes/No
45. Do you often find yourself having to make resolutions to tidy your office, clear your desk, or generally manage time more effectively? Yes/No

You and others

46. Are you able to delegate to colleagues when necessary? Yes/No
47. Do you have ways for (politely) terminating interviews and conversations once you have obtained the information you need? Yes/No
48. Can you help others to stick to the point? Yes/No
49. Do you frequently lose time wondering about other people's motives? Yes/No
50. Do you frequently lose time fuming or fretting after clashes with difficult colleagues or clients? Yes/No
51. Can you say 'no' when necessary, and stick to it? Yes/No
52. When you brief others, do they frequently need to come back to seek clarification or additional information? Yes/No
53. When others brief you, do you frequently need to go back to seek clarification or additional information? Yes/No
54. Are you often engaged in tasks that could be done by people without your qualifications and training? Yes/No
55. Are you often in the position of battling over conflicts of interest with your colleagues? Yes/No
56. Are you confident that you avoid creating unnecessary work for others (some of which will in any case result in more work for you)? Yes/No
57. Have you proper channels of communication for keeping others informed (so that they aren't constantly coming to you with requests for information)? Yes/No
58. Do you inform others of your plans in good time? Yes/No
59. Are you able to deal with interruptions from others courteously but firmly? Yes/No
60. Do you know the people to go to for information and guidance when necessary? Yes/No

covered in the questionnaire, but less able to do so in relation to the other two? Is there one area with which you have obvious difficulty? If it is the first area, *You and your tasks*, this suggests you need to spend time overhauling your working practices. If it is the second area, *You and yourself*, this suggests you may need to work on improving your powers of concentration or memory, or on decision-making. If it is the third area, *You and others*, there may be factors in your professional relationships which need attention.

On the other hand, your time-management problems may appear to be spread relatively evenly over all three areas. Either way, each time you identify a response to one of the questions which in your view reveals an unsatisfactory working practice, ask yourself three questions:

▶ *Why* do I do that, or behave like that with myself or with my tasks or with others?

▶ *What* changes might I be able to make in order to correct this particular unsatisfactory procedure?

▶ *How* can I bring these changes about?

It doesn't matter if you don't have immediate answers to these questions; part of the purpose of this book is to help you find them. The very act of posing these three questions to yourself initiates the process of mental incubation which is often so important in problem-solving. Once we signal to the mind that there is a problem for which we want to find a solution, the mind has a habit of returning to it at both conscious and unconscious levels until this solution emerges. The desire to solve a problem, once it is recognized as being there, seems to be a natural tendency of the human mind, and when it is allied to strong motivation and to the appropriate frame of mind, then the chances of success are good.

Chapter Four

You and Your Tasks

Various attempts have been made by psychologists over the years to classify the way in which people tackle their occupational tasks. For two reasons, none of these classifications can be legitimately generalized right across different working situations. The first reason is that these situations, even within the same profession, differ enormously. The second, and even more important, reason is that people themselves differ.

Thus the most appropriate psychological procedure in this field is not to provide individuals with written tests, the results of which assign them to various work-style categories, and then make dogmatic assertions about these categories. Rather, people should be put in possession of the necessary psychological facts and allowed to work out for themselves what these facts mean in terms of their own working lives. For example, many of us may feel that we tend to work best at tasks which interest us and which we find rewarding. In terms of time-management, this might lead us to draw the very obvious conclusion that in professional life, when people are faced with interesting and rewarding tasks, they are likely to manage their time well. However, this would ignore the fact that it is possible to become so absorbed in such tasks that we pursue peripheral or unimportant details and thus manage time rather badly.

Similarly, we might conclude that when people are faced with uninteresting and unrewarding tasks they will be poor time-managers, but this would ignore the fact that it is possible to work particularly effectively on these tasks, so great is our motivation to get them out of the way and return to those parts of our job which we find more stimulating.

Equally, since most people work best when not under too much pressure and anxiety, this might lead us to conclude that deadlines and time constraints are generally a bad thing. But this would ignore the fact that some individuals positively thrive when faced with such pressures (writers are a good example), and that provided the pressures are not too unrelenting, will actively impose them upon themselves. Generalizations about work-related aspects of the human psychological condition therefore carry certain dangers, and nowhere is this more apparent than in professional life, where the range of tasks which people are called upon to perform can be so great. In consequence, not all the time-management strategies I shall be exploring will apply – or appeal – equally to you. You are the best judge of what is and is not needed in your own time-management programme. So use those which are appropriate for you, and reject (or suitably modify) those which are not.

In thinking over the need to approach time-management in the right frame of mind, you may recognize that there is something in you which is responsible for your resistance to a particular time-management strategy, rather than some inadequacy in the strategy itself. It is still up to you whether you accept the strategy or not, but if you decide against it, do so with a clear understanding of the reason. In time-management training it is of value to identify this reason, as staying with an unsatisfactory way of operating without recognizing why you are doing so can be a major barrier to future progress.

PLANNING YOUR WORKLOAD

SPECIFYING OBJECTIVES

One of the most important questions in *Exercise 4* (page 26) asked whether, when you set out on a task, you have clear objectives as to what you want to achieve. Evidence from psychological research (for example, Pearson and Tweddle, 1984) shows that the existence of clear objectives can be vital for successful performance, and this probably holds good across a wide range of human activity. Objectives identify and stipulate the goals that we wish to achieve, and in managing our workload their presence allows us to:

- identify clearly what needs to be done;
- plan how we are going to do it;
- monitor our progress while we are doing it;
- assess the extent of our success when we have done it;
- learn more effectively from the experiences it has offered us.

To be of real value, objectives should be as specific as possible. Thus, for example, the objective 'To get on top of my paperwork this week' is of much less value than 'By the end of the week to clear urgent outstanding correspondence, to bring (specified) files up-to-date, to write up all my incomplete case studies, and to send off the indents for new equipment'. The first objective is imprecise: I may indeed want to get on top of my paperwork, but I haven't clarified what this will actually involve. The result is that I'll probably either feel overawed by the sheer volume of what seems to be waiting for me and not know where to start, or attack things haphazardly, doing a bit of this and then a bit of that and fail to finish anything properly. The first objective is also open-ended. When will I know that I have succeeded in getting 'on top of my paperwork'? Indeed, is such total success even possible, given that new paperwork will be arriving while I'm attending to the backlog? Open-ended objectives of this kind are not only too vague, but their unattainability can leave us feeling frustrated and, very possibly, inadequate to boot.

By contrast, the second objective is clear and limited: it says exactly what I'm going to do, and no more. It gives me unequivocal guidance on where I'm going to start and where I'm going to finish, and helps me plan what I'm going to do in between. It indicates to me that I must collect together all urgent outstanding correspondence, all relevant documents waiting to be filed, all incomplete case studies, and all the catalogues and indent forms relating to the new equipment. It helps me identify the things I must do in order to deal with all this paperwork, such as booking some secretarial time, looking up my case notes, contacting people who can help me with catalogue queries and so on. It sets me clear achievement targets for the end of the week: Have the outstanding letters been written and posted? Has the filing been done? Are my case studies written up? Have the indents been completed and sent off?

LEARNING FROM SUCCESSES AND FAILURES

A clear objective helps me learn from experience by drawing attention to my specific successes and failures. It may help me identify for example that any attempt to clear a large backlog even of urgent letters in one fell swoop is too much for my powers of literary invention, and that next time I must arrange two shorter sessions with the secretary rather than one long one. And that writing up a backlog of case studies is too much for my powers of memory, even with the help of notes – in future I must resolve to complete them at a set time each week. And that succumbing to the temptation to reread each document before putting it away is a fatal time-waster when filing. In addition I may realize (ruefully) that in future I need to study departmental memos more carefully, as doing so will stop me wasting valuable time by identing for equipment when it has already been announced that funds for the present financial year are exhausted.

WRITING TASK OBJECTIVES

It is unfortunate that outside behavioural psychology itself (a psychology which concentrates upon what people actually do rather than upon the inner world of consciousness), the writing of objectives has had something of a mixed reception. People tend to say things like 'Objectives make everything too inflexible', 'My job is so varied that I can't possibly draw up precise objectives', 'Objectives inhibit creativity', 'I just don't like having to reduce things in that way'. Comments such as these are based upon misconceptions. Far from making things mechanical, objectives often in fact give proper scope for flexibility. To be flexible, we have to have a recognized position from which to *be* flexible. If we have no such position, what looks like flexibility often turns out on closer inspection to be disorganization and lack of proper direction. Similarly with creativity. By its very nature we can't always specify what the ends of creative activity are going to be, but these ends are unlikely to be of much value unless we have some goal at the outset against which our eventual performance can be measured, some particular issue that we want to tackle, or some particular problem that can be defined and that calls for a solution.

The comment on the impossibility of drawing up precise objectives is equally groundless. No matter how varied our job, we can nonetheless identify certain characteristic aspects within it, aspects which are best approached in certain definable ways. If this were not the case, it would be impossible to train people for such a job, and impossible for anyone to improve at it, since past experience would be no guide to the future. And since these characteristic aspects exist, it follows that it is possible to have objectives in relation to them. In fact we have these objectives already, whether we realize it or not. When tackling our work, we all have targets in our minds that we want to achieve, and certain

MANAGEMENT BY OBJECTIVES

The term 'management by objectives' was coined in 1955 by Peter Drucker (Drucker, 1982), and has been part of the vocabulary of management training ever since. Many of the things said and written about management by objectives apply specifically to business managers, rather than to professionals in general, but there are some important points which have bearings upon time-management in whatever area we happen to be working. In brief, these are concerned with:

- the abolition of all unnecessary bureaucracy and red tape;

- an end to any emphasis upon tradition for the sake of tradition (for example, an end to 'But we've always done it that way', 'This has always been our policy');

- the elimination of those aspects of centralized control which cause unnecessary delays at local level;

- an emphasis upon goals rather than upon procedures (that is, upon getting things done rather than upon discussing how to do them).

The management by objectives approach emphasizes that where clear objectives are missing the tendency is to concentrate upon input (how hard people are working) rather than upon output (what they are actually achieving). Thus, in theory, a concentration upon input could lead to an office or department working furiously all day long without a single piece of paper actually entering or leaving the building. Everyone would be so busy creating work for each other that no-one would notice that nothing was really happening. This is the very opposite of *management by objectives*.

ideas as to how to go about achieving our targets. The trouble is that all too often these targets are imprecise and imperfectly formulated, with the result that our work can become unfocused, and unproductive. By clarifying them and making them explicit, we take a major step forward in improving our efficiency and in using our time to better effect.

The reluctance to reduce things to objective terms is also a nonstarter. As I shall suggest in a moment, effective objectives *are* reductionist in that they focus upon behaviour, upon what we actually plan to *do*, rather than allowing us to hide behind vague generalities. And this means they are expressed in concrete language rather than in terms of vague (however well-intentioned) abstractions. But since all jobs involve behaviour of some kind, such objectives are essential if we really want to identify what our behaviour is supposed to achieve. Without concrete objectives and the clear expressions of intention which they involve, our achievements are likely to remain as nebulous as the language which went into the planning of them.

FORMULATING TIME-ON-TASK OBJECTIVES

Objectives can be identified and formulated in all areas of professional life, and they should be regularly reviewed, revised and augmented, with new objectives replacing those that have been achieved. The first step is to draw up an inventory of your objectives, wording them in a way that clarifies exactly what action you intend to take. Following are some more examples of clear objectives related to certain of the issues which *Exercise 4* may have revealed as currently taking up too much of your time. Notice that not only are the objectives direct, but they are also short and simple and refer to particular goals. Objectives which are long and rambling, and which contain a number of vague and disparate goals are not specific enough to focus the mind in ways conducive to success.

Objectives:

- to reduce the time spent travelling each week by at least a third;
- to draw up a list of all important tasks which have avoidably been left unfinished;
- to restrict coffee breaks to 10 minutes;
- to find effective ways of reducing the amount of routine work I take home with me;

- to monitor my use of time more closely by a weekly review of time wasted;

- to clarify the priorities among the various aspects of my job.

Don't worry if your list of objectives becomes rather long, because once you have your list the next step is to place the objectives in order of importance, taking into account the extent to which they are attainable. Some of the objectives that look best on paper may have to be shelved or discarded as being impracticable due to reasons outside your immediate control. Once objectives have been placed in order of priority, you should decide how many can be put into effect initially, and then where possible *make your commitment to them public*. Public commitment has the double value of letting other people know what you intend to do (so that they have more chance to accommodate it), and also of demonstrating your determination to actually do it. None of us enjoy public failure, and this very fact helps to strengthen our motivation. The golden rules when drawing up your objectives are therefore to:

- make them specific;

- ensure they refer to actions;

- keep them short;

- keep them realistic;

- make them public.

ASSIGNING PRIORITIES

Having clarified your objectives, the next step is to place them in order of priority (see Seiwert, 1991). With all objectives, no matter in what area, bear in mind that there are three kinds of priorities, namely priorities of *time*, priorities of *importance*, and priorities of *time and importance*. Some tasks are relatively unimportant, but if they are to be done at all, they must be done urgently if a stipulated deadline is to be met. Others are of more importance, but occupy a more generous time scale. And others are not only important, they are highly urgent.

Obviously the third group, priorities of time and importance, must be dealt with first. But wherever possible the good time-manager tries to clear away tasks before they are allowed to slip into this category. Items in the priorities of time group can be

MAKING YOUR COMMITMENT TO TIME-MANAGEMENT PUBLIC

This can be done in a number of different ways, and the whole issue of relationships with colleagues is looked at in detail in Chapter 6. However, some suggestions are:

- Take the lead in a general drive towards greater working efficiency; put an item on the agenda for the next departmental meeting and prepare a list of suggestions that are likely to benefit everybody. (This is the quickest way of nailing your colours to the mast – people will now expect you to practise what you preach.)

- Make your working schedules public; circulate copies to your colleagues.

- Display (discreetly but obviously) suitable reminders about good time-management on the walls of your office or on your desk; others will soon notice them.

- Allow terms like *time-management* and *working effectiveness* to figure more prominently in your vocabulary.

Once you become more identified with successful time-management, colleagues will come to treat your time with more respect (they will also come to you for advice about improving their own effectiveness, which could mean you lose some of the time you've been working so hard to save – but that's the way of the world).

attended to next, and this often involves making decisions on whether they are worth dealing with at all or whether they can be eliminated from the list. However efficient we are, we can't do everything. Some things have to fall by the wayside. If it's obvious that the deadline associated with an item under priorities of time cannot be met without delaying more important matters, then the task concerned may have to be abandoned or shelved. If this is the case, does this give rise to a smaller, more manageable task such as a letter of apology or a request for more time? If so, this smaller task now becomes a priority in place of the original one.

Items in the remaining group, priorities of importance, must become part of your planning *now*, no matter how much time seems available for dealing with them. If we put them aside, with the vague resolution to deal with them at some indeterminate later date, they'll creep up on us without our noticing, with the result that they will then qualify for the priorities of time and importance list, and have to be dealt with in a panic. The good time-manager tries never to allow items to slip from priorities of importance to priorities of time and importance. I said earlier that some of us like working to deadlines, but if these deadlines are too tight to allow us to deal with something properly, they cannot help but be counterproductive. The human race has always recognized this, as witnessed by the expression 'doing things in *good* time'. To do them in good time means that we give ourselves the space in which to do them properly. To do them in 'bad' time means we do them in a rush and risk making a total mess of them.

One last point. When prioritizing those objectives which are specifically aimed at changing your working practices, the key question to ask yourself is how important each of them is in saving time. Obviously those that carry big time bonuses are likely to be seen as the biggest priorities, but some of those that do not save a great deal of time may be amongst the easiest to achieve. And even a few minutes saved here and there is worth having. So these more humble objectives should, in their different way, also be regarded as priorities to be put into immediate effect.

FORMULATING PLANS FOR ACHIEVING OBJECTIVES

Once your objectives have been identified and placed in order of priority, the next step is to formulate plans for their achievement. Before examining how this can best be done, spend a few minutes

AVOIDING CRISES

Priorities of *time and importance* can all too easily slip into a highly undesirable fourth category, priorities of *crises*. Crises place us under great stress, expose us to the risk of rushed and ill-considered decisions, and force us to shelve other urgent tasks while we deal with them. Good forward planning prevents the great majority of crises from ever arising, and such planning is greatly helped if we learn from those crises which have been allowed to creep up on us. The two vital questions are: '*Why* did the crisis arise?' and '*How* can a similar one be prevented in the future?'

It often goes unrecognized that crises can be great thieves of time. For example, you miss the deadline for posting off an urgent report, and have to spend a whole day rushing somewhere to deliver it by hand. You forget to collect some vital information when the appropriate person is available, and have to spend a whole afternoon desperately trying to track them down in order to get it. You neglect to instruct the porter to prepare the lecture room for an important visiting speaker and to instruct the technician to set up the AV equipment, and have to spend a precious morning doing everything yourself because the appropriate people are currently nowhere to be found.

After experiencing an avoidable crisis, promise yourself that *nowhere*, at *no* time, and under *no* circumstances will you ever allow something like that to happen again.

IDENTIFYING YOUR TIME-ON-TASK OBJECTIVES

EXERCISE 5

Look back at your responses to the first section of the questionnaire contained in *Exercise 4 You and your tasks* (page 26). Identify those responses which indicate to you that your current on-task practices are losing time for you. Select the ones which you consider to be the main culprits (as many or as few as you wish) and write an objective designed to deal with each one of them. Make sure that these objectives conform to the rules laid down earlier (page 36), and be prepared to experiment a little with the wording in order to get them exactly right.

on *Exercise 5*, which is designed to give you some practice in drawing up your own time-on-task objectives.

Now select from the results of *Exercise 5* those objectives which you would like to put into immediate effect. Since the human mind is notorious for 'forgetting' those things that require effort and commitment, it helps if you write these objectives down on separate pieces of card, and keep them where you can see them.

PLANNING

Having clarified your objectives, you can now plan how you are going to achieve them. Don't be tempted to skip this task. Paradoxically, one of the reasons why we fail to manage time effectively is that we don't spend enough time planning exactly how to do so. If this makes time-planning sound like a lengthy chore, I'm misleading you. Even the highest estimates (such as Seiwert, 1991) suggest that only one per cent of any given working period needs to be spent in time-planning in order to produce an average saving of an hour a day. Thus is you are planning the week ahead, you should be prepared to devote about 20 minutes to identifying strategies for time-saving, with a net gain to yourself in working time of over four and a half hours. Since working conditions vary so much, these average figures may not mean much in individual cases, but they do demonstrate that for every minute spent time-planning, many more are usually saved.

I gave examples earlier of how the very act of identifying specific objectives provides us with suggestions as to how we should plan for their achievement, but it is important that the plans be made as specific as the objectives themselves, and *written down*. One approach is to draw up a planning sheet divided into three columns, with objectives listed in the first one, the means towards their achievement in the second, and additional requirements in the third.

Thus, if my objective is to reduce the amount of time I spend travelling to call on clients by at least half, my planning sheet might look like this:

Objective	Means	Additional Requirements
To reduce travelling time by half	Eliminate unneccessary journeys	List wasted journeys made last week
	Combine journeys where possible	Large road map of city
	Choose better routes	Coloured pins to mark home of each client to be visited

With the help of this planning sheet I have reduced the problem to manageable proportions. I have identified clearly what I have to do, and it is now up to me whether or not I do it. If I decide to go ahead, I mark off on the road map the various places I routinely have to visit, using different coloured pins to show which ones I can take in on each particular trip. Now each time I set out to call on a client on, for example, the red pin route, I can anticipate whether there is someone else on the same route who is also due a visit, thus saving me the trouble of having to go out again later in the week.

With my road map, it is also possible to explore whether there are any short cuts on any of the routes that I might be able to use, or any way in which I can avoid traffic bottle-necks. And with the help of the list of wasted journeys I made last week I can ponder how such loss of time can be avoided in the future. Are there certain clients who are clearly unavailable unless I give them prior notice of my visits? Are there others who obviously profit little from my calls, and who therefore can be visited less often in future? And are there clients whose problems can just as well be dealt with by letter or by telephone?

Whether making all these adjustments to my trips actually saves half my travelling time may not be clear until I have put them into effect. And in my case, the figure of one-half may be somewhat arbitrary. But having a definite goal of this kind is much better than the vague resolution 'to save travelling time'. Provided the figure of one-half was based upon a realistic appraisal of some kind rather than simply plucked out of the air, it gives me something definite for which to aim. If after my initial exercise I'm still not saving around one-half of my time, then I can sit down and explore whether the figure should be scaled down or whether there are any additional strategies I can bring into use.

Always assess the effectiveness of your planning in this way. You can learn as much from apparent planning failures as you can from planning successes. If certain plans didn't achieve the desired results, why was this? Was it due to:

▶ *a fault in the plans* (inadequate, unrealistic, inappropriate)?

▶ *a fault in you* (failure to operate them effectively, failure to stick to them)?

▶ *a fault in others* (refusal to co-operate, misunderstanding of what was required of them)?

Even the briefest of plans should be evaluated in this way, and the lesson learnt from it taken to heart and used to enhance future effectiveness.

MISCELLANEOUS TASKS

In a busy professional life there are of course a range of things that crop up which may appear to lie outside the scope of your existing time-planning and time-on-task objectives. Most of these will be non-routine tasks and/or tasks which occur unexpectedly, but you should nevertheless have a consistent overall strategy for dealing with them. Those which cannot be disposed of on the spot should be placed on a formal pending list which is regularly (daily if need be) reviewed and each task assigned to one of the three priority ratings given on page 36. On closer inspection it may become clear that some of the tasks concerned do in fact relate to existing objectives, and they can therefore be linked to these objectives and, where appropriate, to the tasks associated with them. All items remaining on the pending list should be given a date by which they require to be dealt with, and the list handled in accordance with the general strategies for using lists which follow.

GUIDELINES FOR OVERALL TIME-PLANNING

There are a number of guidelines that relate to all aspects of good time-planning, and which should underpin your work in this area. These are now looked at in turn. When reading through these guidelines, try and relate them to the personal time-management objectives that you identified in *Exercise 5*.

WHERE APPROPRIATE, INCLUDE A TIME-FRAME IN YOUR PLANNING
This means that where it is possible to identify how long a task will realistically take, you should specify this in advance and then try to keep to the allotted time. Parkinson's law often operates when a task is undertaken without a time-frame of this kind, and the task thus expands to take up all the time available. Avoid this by specifying the time-frame for each task whenever you can, and identifying (and learning from) the reasons should you find yourself over-running it.

INCLUDE DEADLINES
Even if you can't lay down specific time-frames, always identify the deadline date by which a task has to be completed. Deadlines concentrate the mind, and are a powerful incentive not only to use time productively but also to formalize (organize and structure) the tasks facing you. Deadlines should be realistic but not too generous. If you are too liberal when setting them, all that will happen is that you will leave the work until the last minute, and then find yourself scrambling to complete it, or in the position of having to put the deadline back.

MAKE UP FOR TIME LOSS
If a task overruns its time-frame, or causes you to lose time in other

ways, plan to make up for what you've lost *as soon and as quickly as possible*. This not only means in the immediate future, but also in a concentrated stint rather than over a number of days. The longer you take before making up for lost time, the less likely you are to do so effectively.

INCLUDE REWARDS IN YOUR PLANNING

Managing time effectively is its own reward, but you can greatly help matters along if you build in some extra rewards of your own devising. These work best for our present purposes if they are time-related, so for example you can plan that if you complete the proposed tasks within their allotted time-frame, there will be no need to take work home with you on the weekend and you can then enjoy your leisure time with a clear conscience. If you fail to complete them, the work will have to be taken home and that will put paid to some or all of your weekend. If the work is completed you might want to plan to free a stipulated period of time each afternoon for catching up on more enjoyable tasks from your non-priority list.

Having once set yourself rewards, be sure to obtain them only if your objectives *are* met. This not only allows your rewards to retain their effect, it also helps your powers of self-discipline, powers which are important in putting into effect any successful time-management programme.

MAKE YOUR PLANS AS SPECIFIC AS POSSIBLE

Just as time-management objectives must be as specific as possible, so must the plans that support them. For example, if your objective is to gather information from colleagues or from other professionals about a particular client who is causing you concern, your plans should not take the form of vague reminders like 'contact Dr Smith about X', but indicate exactly *how* and *when* Dr Smith will be contacted, and exactly *what* will be discussed with him or her. Thus you might write down:

Phone Dr Smith 10 a.m. Wednesday (a time when you know Dr Smith is available) *and ask for details of X's employment record.*

In this way you avoid several fruitless attempts to contact Dr Smith (the kind of attempts that are made on the spur of the moment just when the need to make them happens to cross your mind), and equally importantly, you avoid discussing irrelevant issues with him or her or perhaps even forgetting altogether the real reason for making the contact until after you've put down the phone.

PLAN TO SET ASIDE BLOCKS OF TIME WHENEVER YOU CAN

Time is always spent more efficiently if you can allocate it in blocks rather than in several short bursts. Thus an hour spent on a task usually allows more to be done than three fragments of 20 minutes or so spread over several days. Fragmenting time means that we usually waste precious minutes picking up the threads of a task each time we return to it – we have to remember where we left off last time, refresh our mind on the salient facts and put out of our heads thoughts connected with the last task on which we were working. We may also lose time getting out the necessary papers, requesting the help of a colleague, and so on. In addition, the human mind rarely works at its best when it is having to turn constantly from one task to another, without concentrating properly on any one of them.

Of course, the boredom factor has to be taken into account. It is unproductive to allocate a substantial period of time for a particular task if we know perfectly well that the task is so dull it is impossible to concentrate effectively upon it for that long. But our own experience should allow us to strike the right balance between the need to block time and the need to stay fresh while we're working.

PLAN TO GROUP TASKS

This raises issues similar to those associated with blocking time. Constantly flitting from one type of task to another not only risks leaving half of them unfinished, but can prevent the mind from operating on anything other than a superficial level. Grouping tasks on the other hand allows a greater concentration of thought and of effort, and where appropriate can mean that we save time by using the same facilities to cope with all of them.

CONCENTRATE ON A LIMITED NUMBER OF TASKS

Trying to do too many things at once even when tasks of a similar nature are grouped together, is a major cause of inefficiency and of occupational stress. Insist, both to yourself and to colleagues, that you focus your attention on a limited number of tasks until they are finished before you move on to others. Don't allow yourself to become too distracted. Since we can only take one step at a time in life, make sure that each step is forward and not sideways – or worse still, backwards!

PLAN TO DELEGATE

Delegation is such an important part of a good time-management programme that I will return to it in greater detail in Chapter 6. I mention it here because it is often an important aspect of forward planning.

PLAN WHAT HAPPENS WHEN YOU ARE AWAY

One of the major problems of time-management encountered by many in professional life is the expectation that they can be in two places at once. Thus, when they're out of the office, work continues to arrive on their desks just as if they were still there, resulting in a constant struggle to catch up with a backlog of tasks. This can be partly avoided by delegation (if you're in that happy position), or by arranging with colleagues that you will cover for each other. If there is a secretary who can take telephone calls for you, make sure that they have a telephone logbook in which each incoming call is recorded together with the time it arrived (often vital information but just as often neglected), the name of the caller, the purpose of the call, and the action (if any) which needs to be taken as a result.

For the telephone logbook to be operated effectively, arm the secretary with a brief list of questions to put to each caller in order to elicit these items of information. Most of these questions are obvious enough, but particular attention should be paid to those relating to any action which may need to be taken. For example, if the caller asks you to ring back, they should be requested to give times when it will be convenient for you to do so. Alternatively, they can be given a time to ring again which is suitable for you. If the caller wants to arrange a meeting, they should be asked to suggest more than one possible date, and indicate roughly how long the meeting is likely to last. If they want information, they can be invited to put their request in writing, as people are much less verbose on paper than they are on the telephone.

Another important piece of help you can request, if you are likely to be away for more than a day, is that your mail is sorted into separate bundles and placed on your desk instead of being left in an untidy heap or stuffed into your pigeon hole.

Departmental memos can go in one bundle, internal mail in another, official mail in another, personal mail in another, and so on. This only takes a minute or two for whoever brings in the mail each day, and it not only provides you with a less daunting prospect when you return (half the battle in getting started on a job is to make sure it doesn't look too intimidating in the first place), but allows you to more easily group the tasks (see page 45) involved in dealing with your mail. Whoever sorts the mail should also be asked to put the most recent items to the bottom (with the exception of anything marked urgent), so that you can scan through them in the order in which they were received.

Most important of all, plan ahead for any lengthy absence from the office. Go carefully through the things that need to be done between now and then, and give each of them a time-frame. Make a list of the key people who need to be informed that you will be away, and send out a brief duplicated note to each of them, giving the dates of your absence and, if possible, the name of someone who can be contacted in your place. Identify any deadlines which may fall due while you are away, and either bring them forward or arrange to have them put back. List any of your books or documents that others are going to need in your absence, and make sure they know where to find them. Lock up everything else – time spent locating items of property 'borrowed' by colleagues while you're away is time very badly spent.

PLAN TO AVOID UNNECESSARY MEETINGS
Meetings are the biggest thief of time of all (remember Mintzberg's finding quoted on page 18 that nearly 70 per cent of a manager's time is spent in meetings.) A two-hour meeting attended by 20 people gobbles up 40 hours (more than one working week) of prime professional time. You can work out for yourself how much public or corporation money it swallows (the average hourly salary of the people present + 70 per cent for overhead costs of an individual's employment, multiplied by the number of people present). And this is only part of the story. We also have to add travelling time and costs if people are coming from a distance, and often the 'dead' time on either side of a meeting. (For example it is difficult to use the brief intervals before and after a meeting which takes up most of the afternoon, even supposing such intervals aren't spent by participants in debate and recriminations sparked off by the meeting, or in licking the wounds inflicted by it).

Some meetings are essential of course, but just as many are not. Those that *are* essential could usually be over and done with in half the time. I could suggest that you always plan to be away on vital business when meetings are scheduled, but this is unrealistic. Experience shows that from the very meetings we don't attend come the worst decisions. But meetings aren't always called by other people – we may be the culprit ourselves sometimes. So whenever you find yourself planning a meeting, ask yourself:

▶ Is it a substitute for action? (If so, act instead of meeting.)

▶ Is there a less time-consuming way of getting the business done? (For example, phone calls, faxes, e-mail, memos asking for a response by a given date if recipients want their ideas taken into account. (See Christie and Kingan, 1977, for other possibilities.)

▶ If we must meet, how can I involve as few people as possible? (Their time is precious as well as mine, and the fewer inessential people present, the less unnecessary debate there will be.)

▶ Is the meeting for *discussion* or *decision*? (If the former, a discussion document should be circulated in advance so that people have time to prepare; if the latter, agenda items should make clear the specific decisions that need to be taken.)

▶ Has the meeting a time-frame? (Even the most well-conducted meetings may overrun, but there should nearly always be a target time for concluding, which should be made clear before the meeting begins, and backed up by a public statement of the approximate minute-by-minute cost of holding it.

When the meeting is over, be sure to circulate to each participant a summary of what was decided (in formal meetings this is taken care of by the minutes). If certain individuals have been asked by the meeting to take action in certain areas, make sure they are named in this summary, and the date given on which they are expected to report back. This clarifies the nature of the action concerned and emphasizes the names of those responsible for carrying it out.

What about meetings which you have to attend but which are not of your own arranging? Most of us groan when we receive the agenda, and forget about it until the time of the meeting actually arrives. However, a few minutes spent planning exactly what you want to emerge from the meeting, and the points you want to raise in the course of it, can produce enormous dividends. Write each of

CONDUCTING A MEETING

Being a good chairperson involves not only helping a meeting to come to decisions, but also ensuring that it takes up no more time than is necessary. Good chairpersons typically ensure that:

- only relevant items are included on the agenda (and all relevant documents are circulated before the meeting);

- *procedural wrangles* are resolved *before* the meeting wherever possible, not *during* it;

- where procedural wrangles are still likely to arise, the chair is better informed than anyone else on all relevant rules, regulations and precedents;

- the meeting starts on time, whether everyone is present or not;

- all speakers keep to the agenda; where irrelevancies are introduced the chair intervenes politely but firmly. (For example 'That's an interesting point, but it could be dealt with informally by the people concerned'; 'We covered that issue at our last meeting and I can't allow us to go back over it'; 'If you want that discussed, could you put it on the agenda for our next meeting?');

- the chair summarizes often, usually as a preliminary to asking for proposals;

- a time-limit is set for discussion on lengthy items; if for good reason it has to be exceeded, the chair summarizes and insists that the discussion now focuses only upon specific proposals;

- everyone talks though the chair, and the chair quickly lowers the temperature if disputes develop between participants – as a last resort suspending the item concerned;

- the meeting is reminded when necessary of the cost per minute of holding it.

In addition, the good chairperson has techniques for dealing with the various kinds of people who are likely to be troublesome at meetings, such as the compulsive talker (the meeting is invited to comment on what they are saying), the aggressive individual (they are asked if they have a firm proposal), the negative individual (they are asked to supply facts and figures), the offensive individual (their remarks are decisively ruled out of order).

these down. In the heat sometimes generated by meetings it is all too easy to lose sight of them, and end up kicking yourself afterwards for doing so. At the same time, look up any facts and figures that will prove useful to you when stating your case (few things impress others more readily or win more votes than relevant facts and figures). Also ask yourself whether it is worth putting something on paper for circulation at the meeting (something else which impresses others, most of whom will have come to the meeting without any preparation at all).

PLAN TO HAVE NECESSARY FACILITIES READILY AVAILABLE
Much prime task-time is lost hunting for information or seeking reference material. It goes without saying that it is imperative to keep necessary addresses and telephone numbers readily to hand (see Chapter 6), but there is a great deal of other material that we ought also to have instantly available. How often do we find ourselves saying 'I really must get a copy of that' about some reference book or other, only to forget about it until the next time we need the information that it contains?

When setting out your objectives and planning for them, note down the type of facilities that will help in their achievement. If you need to request such facilities through departmental or corporation funds, you stand most chance of success if you can cost *clearly* the time that having them will save you (for example, work out the cost in time and money of the trips made over the past year in order to consult elsewhere the essential reference material you feel should be in your possession, or work out the savings in time of a new computer programme or updated equipment). It is surprising how often people omit this elementary strategy when making bids for whatever money is available in the capital fund. The very fact that you have taken the time to cost out benefits in this way (provided it is done accurately) impresses those who control the purse strings, if only because it is so rare for anyone to go to this kind of trouble. Even where benefits in time and money cannot be quantified, at the very least the other advantages accruing from your proposed purchases should be listed in detail, and wherever possible the names given of all those who will benefit from them besides yourself.

PLAN TO FIND THINGS
The case study of Brian in Chapter 3 gave an example of the time that can be lost simply hunting for things apparently mislaid. The

conviction that we put an important document in a 'safe place' is no guarantee that we will be able to find it again when we want it. A good filing system, kept up-to-date, is an essential safeguard against time lost in hunting, but by itself it isn't sufficient. We may often file things and fail to remember under which heading we've filed them. In addition, we're bombarded each day by miscellaneous items which we need to put aside briefly without actually assigning them to a file (memos, notes from colleagues, telephone messages, sales leaflets, audio and video tapes, computer print-outs, forms, offprints). Then there are the pieces of hardware that are in constant use but are never to hand when we want them (keys are amongst the worst offenders).

It is a fact of life that the human memory just isn't up to the task of remembering the minutiae of working life of which these things are an inevitable part. We need therefore to have an allotted place even for, indeed especially for, things in constant use, and to discipline ourselves always to put them back in their place, even though we know we are going to need them again shortly. But many of the things that come our way are destined only for a short stay, and human memory being what it is, we put them down and five minutes later have forgotten completely what we did with them.

The solution is absurdly simple. Keep a notebook on your desk (a spare diary is ideal, as it allows things to be entered by date) and *write down* where you put these short-stay items. There may only be two or three entries each day, taking a matter of seconds each, but the saving in time and frustration is little short of miraculous (though make sure the notebook stays on your desk, otherwise it could well join the list of things for which you spend half your life hunting).

It also helps enormously if you make a point of *clearing* your desk at the end of each working day (one dose of my own medicine that I find almost impossible to swallow).

PLAN TO THROW THINGS AWAY

I know that it's the very thing you threw away yesterday that you find you need today. But trying to keep everything that may come in useful at some indeterminate time in the future leads inevitably to a cluttered office, and to filing cabinets full of bulging and yellowing papers that no one is ever going to look at. Hanging on to things unnecessarily is often a sign of psychological insecurity. Whenever possible, make decisions at the point of arrival of items as to what is, and what is not, to be kept. If you find this difficult, plan to have at regular intervals a day or half-day when you go through everything and decide what can go into the wastepaper basket. Be ruthless. The question to ask about each item is, 'What's the worst that could happen if I don't keep this?' You'll be surprised at how often the answer is 'next to nothing', and each time it is, throw it away. (Mintzberg, 1979, found for example that only 13 per cent of the mail received by his sample of managers was of specific and immediate use.)

When you've carried out this exercise and got rid of a lot of junk, note how you feel. People sometimes report that the process is rather like a purification ritual. By clearing the room of rubbish, they have the feeling of having also cleared their minds. This is not surprising. After all, your office is in a way a projection of yourself, and as such it becomes a part of your identity. Ridding it of the dead encumbrances of the past rids your mind of some of them at the same time. If you like, look upon it as a symbolic act of renewal, like the spring-clean that follows winter.

PLAN TO USE LISTS EFFECTIVELY

Lists are an indispensable part of the professional's working life, yet few of us use them properly. We scribble them on scraps of paper (which we then usually lose), and are forever making new ones and having to transfer items from the old. The best lists are those which are *formalized* and which contain only *short-term items* which get done as soon as possible and are not endlessly carried forward to future lists. Let us take these two points in turn.

Formalizing lists means that the items they contain are categorized under relevant headings instead of entered haphazardly. Work out the categories appropriate to you (keep them brief – for example *Speak to, Telephone, Despatch, Complete, Write to, Order*) and type them at the head of a conveniently sized sheet of paper. Make photocopies, and spiral-bind them to form a notebook. As items crop up, enter them in the appropriate column, underlining those that are top priority. The use of columns not only allows you to see much more clearly what needs to be done, it also allows you to group tasks together. If you have several phone calls to make, set aside an interval in which you can get as many of them out of the way as possible. If you have several things to despatch, spend a block of time getting all of them ready for the post. If you have a number of letters to write, do as many as possible together.

Review your list daily, and bring forward items so that they do not become buried in earlier pages. However, confining your list to *short-term* items means that anything which is brought forward more than once or twice has no place on it. Such items fall into one of two categories. Either they are *non-urgent*, in which case they should be transferred to your longer-term objectives rather than allowed to feature on your list, or you are *procrastinating* over them, in which case you have the choice of either discarding them or of doing them *now*.

PLAN TO PROTECT YOURSELF
Interruptions during the working day not only take up time, but they also steal precious minutes while you pick up the threads of your work again after they're over. Some of them are unavoidable, but many are not. Don't feel guilty about protecting yourself from the more unnecessary or inconvenient ones (see also Chapter 6). If you have a secretary, he or she can indicate to callers when you are and when you are not available, but in the absence of a secretary, publish a list of the times when people can see you without an appointment. Be as generous as possible with these blocks of time. If you are miserly with them you are not only unfair to others, but you will soon have a backlog of individuals clamouring for your attention.

Blocking time in this way is another example of the golden rule of *grouping* your tasks wherever possible. The great majority of people will respect that this is what you are doing, and will co-operate accordingly. Anyone who fails to do so can hardly grumble when you politely remind them that they have come at the wrong time, and suggest they come back later.

PLAN TO CUT DOWN ON PAPERWORK
Part of the problem is that people have far too little respect for paper and for the trees from which it comes. As a writer, I have for as long as I can remember enjoyed the feel and look of paper, in much the same way I would imagine that a painter enjoys the feel and look of a canvas. It therefore grieves me to see in professional life (to say nothing of daily life) so much of it covered by unedifying nonsense. I have more to say about this when discussing communication with colleagues in Chapter 6, but in all contexts the good time-manager tries to cut down on the amount of unnecessary attention given to paperwork, and on the amount of unnecessary clutter it is often allowed to create.

In my own professional life I have to confess that I sometimes find myself at meetings having thrown away the vital papers that those around me are self-righteously pulling from their briefcases, but the odd lapse of this kind is more than compensated for by the feeling of relief when sheaves of unwanted documents thud into the wastepaper basket. In order to deal effectively with paperwork, a definite (and sustainable) policy is vital. One good approach is to have a set routine for dealing with each category of incoming material. For example:

Memos – record immediately in the appropriate place any important information which they contain, such as dates for your diary. This allows 90 per cent of them to be thrown away.

Brochures – throw away the irrelevant ones, pass the others to colleagues or file them away for future use. *Don't* be tempted to browse through them out of curiosity now.

Questionnaires – pity the poor researchers before discarding, but if you do decide to fill them in, do so at once or take them home and complete them that evening. Don't allow them to clutter up your files just to salve your conscience, and then feign regret when you miss the deadline for returning them.

Letters – keep a supply of large compliments slips and scribble quick replies to all routine mail requiring only acknowledgement of receipt. Record necessary information and addresses (as for memos), then discard unless there is a good reason for filing. Reply to urgent letters *now*; never allow others to become buried at the bottom of your in-tray; keep your own replies brief and to the point. If your recipient is in the habit of claiming not to have received important letters, use recorded delivery (but in any case always record in a notebook the date on which letters are sent, and to whom).

Reports – if they're important, clip a sheet of paper to the front and write on it 'Main Points', summarizing these briefly in your own words underneath. If there are too many of them for this, write down the page numbers on which these main points occur; if the reports are unimportant and no use to colleagues, use them for scrap paper or feel grateful to the person who empties your wastepaper basket.

Journals – note any of the articles you feel you should read (mercifully few in many cases), clip a card to the front cover with page numbers, then put the journal away until you can give the articles your proper attention. Don't be tempted to start dipping into them now, unless you want to lose half your morning.

Agendas of meetings – note any items for which you need to prepare, and do your preparation as soon as possible; don't leave it until the day before the meeting. Make sure that the date of the meeting is in your diary.

Minutes of meetings – read through and send an *immediate* note to the secretary concerning anything which you feel has been incorrectly reported, anything relating to matters arising, and anything which you want to put on the agenda for the next meeting; then file.

OFFICE MACHINERY

One of the best aids of all in dealing with paperwork is, of course, the word processor. I always advise people in professional life to learn not only how to use one but also how to type properly, thus allowing them to make much better use of it. The time taken in mastering both these tasks will reward you a hundredfold every year in time saved. The word processor allows you to store much of your own material on disc rather than in a bulging filing cabinet. You can also store standard paragraphs for use in official correspondence on disc, and use them as needed. Even though you may have your own secretary, it is often much quicker to type your written work straight into the word processor rather than dictate it and then be faced with reading it through, correcting the result and then checking the final copy. An added advantage is that this releases your secretary to carry out other delegated tasks for you, which in turn will save you more time.

A word processor (or a computer programme) also allows you to store a mine of other information – lists of your files, of your appointments, of case notes, of student marks and grades and so on – and call them up at the touch of a button. If you are much involved in writing, the benefits of a word processor in terms of increased effectiveness and efficiency are incalculable. This is not the place to list everything it can do for you, but suffice it to say that from tomorrow, if you don't already use one, I advise you to start finding out how to do so.

Similar advice can be given in respect to the range of other office machinery now available. It is a mistake to see such machinery as the exclusive concern of a secretary or a technician, and to imagine that specialist knowledge if needed in order to use it. A laptop computer, provided it is compatible with the machines used in the office, is a major boon, since it allows you to put material on disc at home or while on time-wasting train journeys and business trips, which can then be edited and printed on your return. Modems, which can be added on to office computers, allow you to make direct contact via the telephone network with similarly equipped computers in other offices, thus allowing you to take advantage of electronic mail (e-mail) and to access suitable data bases held elsewhere. Sometimes such facilities can be used as effective and efficient alternatives to business meetings (see page 48), and are ideal for the rapid dissemination of information to relevant parties.

Fax machines are another time saver, allowing you to send and receive facsimiles of documents in a fraction of the time it would take were they to go by post. Answer-phones can also be a great asset, enabling you to receive information while out of the office. If you are using an answer-phone, be sure to leave an appropriate instructional message for in-coming callers. A general instruction to the caller to leave his or her name and telephone number, and a blanket promise to ring the person concerned back as soon as you can, may only involve you in making a number of non-urgent (and often unanswered) calls. Word your message instead so that it asks callers to state what topic they want to discuss with you, and to give a time when they can guarantee to be available, should they wish you to call them back.

'THERE MUST BE A BETTER WAY'

There is a maxim frequently used in the context of social psychology (that branch of psychology which has to do with social interactions and social structures) which is relevant to all aspects of time-management, namely 'There must be a better way'. There must be a better way than the one we're using at present. There must be a more effective way of relating, of planning, of identifying priorities. And indeed there must. The more we examine our present procedures the more we identify how wasteful they are of precious time. Most of our working procedures in professional life develop somewhat haphazardly; new tasks are added to our workload virtually every day, old tasks change their form or drop out of the reckoning, fresh regulations are introduced and existing ones superseded, working conditions are changed and then changed again, new facilities and equipment become available and existing ones disappear, and so it goes on. To add to it all, we develop new skills and acquire new knowledge. Yet we rarely, if ever, take the time to give our job a thorough overhaul, and see how we can organize it so that our time is used more effectively and potentially more enjoyably. So the maxim 'There must be a better way' is a useful one to remember. Don't bemoan the fact that you don't have enough hours in the day to get things done. Instead, better organize the hours you do have. When you've done so, you might just be surprised at how elastic they can become.

Chapter Five

You and Yourself

If you look back at your responses to the 'You and yourself' section of *Exercise 4* (page 27), you will see that many of the problems which you may have with managing time are related to your own psychology. Learning to manage time not only means learning strategies for organizing and planning our professional tasks, it also means learning to change things in ourselves. And once the changes are effected, it means we must use rather more self-discipline in order to monitor ourselves and make sure these changes are maintained.

As a first step in bringing about the necessary changes, complete *Exercise 6*.

IDENTIFYING SELF-OBJECTIVES

EXERCISE 6

Select from the section on 'You and yourself' in *Exercise 4* those aspects of yourself which you consider to be the main culprits in your unsatisfactory time-management (select as many or as few as you wish) and write an objective designed to deal with each in turn.

Make sure that these objectives conform to the rules laid down on page 36 of Chapter 4, and be prepared to experiment a little with the wording in order to get them exactly right.

The objectives which you have listed relate specifically to yourself, but many of them will be common to most of us, as we will see in the case of Marian, a university lecturer.

❏ *Marian: a case study in time lost through psychological factors*
Marian is a very gifted woman who obtained a first-class honours degree in economics followed by a Ph.D. three years later. After a one-year postdoctoral fellowship she obtained a lecturer's post in her own university, which she has now held for six years. She is a committed and conscientious teacher, liked and respected by both her students and her colleagues. But she says of herself:

'I'm becoming more and more anxious at my inability to get things done, particularly any real writing. I published three papers on my Ph.D. research, and two more on areas arising from it, but I've completed nothing now for nearly four years, and although I've made several starts on a book I've been commissioned to write, I've never got beyond drafting and redrafting the first chapter. My head of department asked me to submit a proposal this year for research money, but I missed the deadline for sending it in.

I'm a good teacher, and I like my work. I serve on several committees, and do my fair share of departmental administration. I'm always busy, and I rarely have an evening or a weekend free of work. But I never have much to show for my efforts. I'm always surrounded by things that are half-finished. I've been trying to rewrite my undergraduate syllabuses for the past six months, I've been trying to complete a study guide for my research students, I've got three books waiting to be reviewed for various journals, I've got letters to answer, I've got a conference report that's long overdue, and I'm still dithering about whether I can afford the time to accept an invitation to teach abroad during the coming summer vacation. I'm 32 next year, and I can't go on being young and promising for ever'.

Marian's problem is not that she can't work hard. Nor is it that she is unable to set her time-on-task priorities. She has mentioned several of these – to publish more in academic journals, to get down to her book, to finish rewriting her undergraduate syllabuses, to write her book reviews and to complete her conference report. And she has proved that she does possess the ability to organize her work by her success as an undergraduate and as a research student (though in both instances she says she recognizes her debt to her tutors who set deadlines for her and pushed her to meet them). Her problems have much more to do with herself. In answering the kind of questions contained in *Exercise 4* she established for example that she:

- tends to put her priorities off until later, and to focus instead on minor matters;
- creates extra work for herself;
- rarely seems able to relax;
- is slow in making decisions;
- often becomes bogged down in details;
- frequently makes resolutions to use time more effectively (a sure sign that she never carries any of them out for long).

It is tempting to suppose that once Marian identified these shortcomings in herself, all she had to do was resolve to remedy them and set her objectives accordingly. But life isn't that easy. Resolutions which relate to our own psychology are much easier to make than to keep. They may require quite fundamental changes to the way we think about ourselves and our lives, and at times may touch upon quite deep-seated aspects of our personality. But there were two steps which Marian was able to take which greatly helped her in keeping her resolutions.

NOTING THE BENEFITS OF GOOD TIME-MANAGEMENT

Firstly, along the lines of the advice given in Chapter 4, she determined to take careful account of the rewards and benefits which putting these resolutions into effect brought her. Many of the advantages which accrue from good time-management in professional life (especially in a job such as Marian's) are not immediately evident unless you make a deliberate point of looking for them. For example, even with good time-management, progress on Marian's book was still slow, but at least there was progress. She noted her feeling of satisfaction as she met each of the weekly deadlines she had set herself for her book, and each week she printed out the completed pages from her word processor so that she could see them grow. She kept a note of how many hours a week she spent on routine work taken home with her, and kept a graph to show that over the weeks the trend was steadily downwards. She noted the reduced time she had to spend correcting the work of her research students once she had given them her study guide, and so on.

In addition to these immediate rewards, Marian also built in some secondary rewards, as recommended in Chapter 4. For example, she built in some flexible time at the weekend, which she allowed herself to use as she pleased if she reached the targets. If she didn't reach her targets, this time had to be used for work. If this sounds as if Marian left herself with scant time for leisure, let me reassure you that good time-management produces *more* real leisure time rather than less. Before beginning her time-management programme Marian was 'always busy', rarely had 'an evening or a weekend completely free of work', and in spite of everything was constantly 'surrounded by things that are half-finished'. Hardly a recipe for real leisure time! Even when she did try to take time off, she couldn't relax because she was always thinking of the things that needed doing and feeling guilty that she wasn't doing them. So she was remaining on-task even when nominally off-task or between tasks. However, once the time-management programme was properly under way, she found that not only did she have more time to herself, but she was able to enjoy it with a clear conscience and had more energy when she did get back to work.

It was only possible for Marian to monitor self-improvement as closely as this and sustain her motivation because the time-management objectives she had set herself adhered to the rules set out in Chapter 4. Thus, with her book, she looked ahead, took into account all her commitments, worked out what represented a reasonable output of written words each week, and set small but realistic weekly objectives accordingly. As a result of the pleasure she felt in meeting these objectives, she became increasingly committed to them, and began to protect her time more zealously from unnecessary encroachments (for example she resigned from some of the committees on which she was serving). With her new undergraduate syllabuses she set herself the deadline of completing them in time for presentation to the next meeting of the Board of Studies, and asked the secretary to put it on the published agenda. With her book reviews she promised to buy herself another new book on the completion of each one.

Marian doesn't pretend that any of this was particularly easy, but she has surprised herself at how quickly she has become accustomed and committed to her new and more effective way of life. She confesses now to looking back on her old self with a mixture of amazement and pity: 'How on earth did I manage to get myself into that kind of mess, and wallow in it for six precious years?'

IDENTIFYING THE REASONS FOR POOR TIME-MANAGEMENT

Marian's question is a good one. I said earlier that there were two steps that Marian was able to take to help her keep her resolutions to manage time effectively. The first was noting the benefits of good time-management. Asking the question of how she had managed to get into this situation was the second of them. In answering it, Marian identified the big difference between working hard and getting things done. The former simply demands effort, the latter demands we recognize in ourselves all the things (subtle and otherwise) that give rise to our poor time-management habits, and thus come between us and the effective use of our own abilities. It demands, in fact, that we study ourselves in the way in which we would study any other instrument with which we have to work. After all, if you bought an expensive piece of equipment, you would familiarize yourself with all its workings by getting to know the owner's manual before you tried using it. It isn't too much to ask you to do the same with yourself. Exercise 7 is a light-hearted exercise that helps to emphasize this point, and it was one which helped Marian answer her own question.

WRITING AN OWNER'S MANUAL

EXERCISE 7

Imagine you are writing an owner's manual giving guidance on how best you can be used at work. Don't take the exercise too seriously, but try to give an accurate picture of how an owner could get the best out of you. That means identifying not necessarily what would make your life unrealistically easy, but how you can be put to most productive use. Be as objective as possible, and indicate the situations in which, and the conditions under which, you can be made to function best. Use your responses to the 'You and Yourself' section of *Exercise 4* to help you if need be. They may indicate some of the things against which the owner should be on guard!

What does this exercise demonstrate to you? Perhaps that up to now you have been neglecting some of the most important points

You and Yourself / 63

in the manual: Or perhaps that you don't really know the conditions under which you operate most productively, and so your manual is in consequence maddeningly inadequate. Either way, use the exercise to help you think about those personal characteristics which may currently be hindering you in your attempts to manage time more effectively. In the remainder of this chapter we will look at the things that can be done to modify or change some of these personal characteristics, and it is for you to decide which of them apply in particular to you.

A POSITIVE APPROACH

Marian's owner' manual contained references to some of the things we've already identified as important in her case. For example, she wrote down:

Her attention must continually be drawn back to her priorities, and she must be prevented from becoming sidetracked by minor matters or immersed in too much detail.

She must always be clear about what she intends to do, and she must be made to keep a careful record of the benefits that come from good time-management.

She must not be allowed to procrastinate, to make excuses for herself, or to use routine work as an excuse for not getting down to something more creative.

On the other hand, she must be encouraged to take a positive approach to herself and to her abilities.

The item upon which Marian laid most emphasis was the final one, 'she must be encouraged to take a positive approach to herself and to her abilities'. I referred to the importance of positive thinking in Chapter 2, and Marian was in no doubt about the vital role it must play in her life in future. In spite of her past academic successes, she recognized in herself a lack of real confidence in her own abilities. If something never quite gets finished, then it never has to be submitted to the test of success or failure. We can always comfort ourselves with the thought that if it *were* to be finished it would be good. While we persist in this kind of thinking, then nothing that exposes us to the critical judgement of ourselves or of others *will* get finished. The problem is that we are not really prepared to back ourselves. Marian was able to achieve well as an undergraduate and as a research student, when her tutors were praising her and formulating her objectives for her, thus providing her with confidence and acting as her motivators. But once she no longer had the support of her tutors and found herself having to rely on self-confidence and self-motivation, her courage started to fail her. Her protestations that she couldn't find time to finish her research papers or get on with her book properly were really excuses for her negative thinking about herself. And, of course, the more she failed to finish anything, the more this negative thinking was being reinforced. Had she continued like this, she would have become increasingly locked into her vicious circle of 'I'm no good therefore I can't finish anything → I can't finish anything therefore I'm no good'.

The solution for Marian lay in changing this self-defeating pattern of thinking. Frequently the main cause of failure in people of Marian's proven ability is not that their work is no good but that they lack the self-confidence to put it to the test. Even Marian's failure to complete the rewriting of her undergraduate syllabuses was due to the fear that her colleagues would criticize them, and that (even more importantly) she would lack the self-belief to stand up to them. Marian could not give herself more confidence overnight, but she recognized that this confidence would only (could only) come as a result of managing her time better, completing her tasks, and tasting the success that this brings. But the place to start was with the simple but highly effective rule that each time she found herself procrastinating over one of her tasks she must remember to ask herself 'What would a self-confident person do now?' And whenever the answer was 'Sit down and get this work finished,' then that is exactly what she had to do. In this way, Marian began behaving as a self-confident person would behave. This behaviour helped her to start producing the results that a self-confident person would produce, thus quickly building up the strength of her self-belief. She was replacing her vicious circle with a virtuous one of 'I'm good therefore I can finish things → I can finish things therefore I'm good'.

Marian's ability to respond in this way led her to stop agonizing over what might or might not be the outcome of her work – in other words she recognized when to switch from being *outcome-centred* to being *task-centred*. It is appropriate to be outcome-centred when setting objectives and when assessing final performance, but during the performance itself one needs to be task-centred. To be task-centred is to put your attention and energy wholly into what it is you have to do. To be outcome-centred at such a time is to waste energy speculating on what the responses to your completed work are likely to be before you've even completed it. Time enough to think about outcomes when the work is actually finished, and you come to look over it and carry out any necessary editing or correcting. Agonizing about the outcome while work is still in progress can not only fuel your fear of failure, it can also destroy concentration and contribute towards the very results that you fear.

BE REALISTIC

Fear of failure can also be linked to perfectionism. We're so concerned about what others will think of our finished efforts that we go to endless pains to get them absolutely right, and not only squander time unnecessarily but also risk killing off our spontaneity and creativity in the process. Obviously it's poor time-management to do things badly and then have to do them all over again, but perfectionism stems from the erroneous belief that the more time we spend on something the better it is bound to be. Such a belief ignores the law of diminishing returns, which in the context of time-management is most precisely expressed in the *Pareto Time Principle*, or the *80:20 Principle*.

Named after the Italian economist Vilfredo Pareto (1848–1923), this principle states that within any system the tendency is for some constituent elements to yield much higher returns than others, with 20 per cent of the total elements being high yielders and 80 per cent low, and the high yielders producing 80 per cent of the total returns while the low yielders produce only 20 per cent. Thus, for example, 20 per cent of a factory's products (or 20 per cent of the components of these products or 20 per cent of the time spent making them) frequently yield 80 per cent of the profits, 20 per cent of the workforce frequently do 80 per cent of the productive work, and so on. Conversely, 80 per cent of the products may yield only 20 per cent of the profits, and 80 per cent of the workforce do only 20 per cent of the productive work.

The *Pareto Time Principle* is claimed also to apply to the production of less desirable results. For example, 20 per cent of the participants in a meeting are likely to monopolize 80 per cent of the time, 20 per cent of clients to produce 80 per cent of the headaches. Conversely 80 per cent of the participants in a meeting are likely to take up only 20 per cent of the time, 80 per cent of the clients to give only 20 per cent of the headaches. (Note that in these examples the 20 per cent who monopolize things won't necessarily be the most useful participants, or the 20 per cent who give headaches the most deserving clients.)

Research appears to show that the *Pareto Time Principle* may hold good across a wide range of areas (Seiwert, 1991). In terms of time-management and productivity it implies that 20 per cent of the time you spend on something is likely to produce 80 per cent of your final output, while the remaining 80 per cent of your time will only achieve 20 per cent of it. Even in such idiosyncratic activities as writing it still tends to apply, with some 20 per cent of your time given over to surges of inspiration in which 80 per cent of the work is done, and 80 per cent spent on the revising, editing, pencil chewing and cursor watching which accounts for the remaining 20 per cent.

Obviously there is nothing fixed about the 80:20 ratio. In the case of extreme procrastinators, time-wasters and perfectionists, the ratio between high yield and low yield time may be very much worse than 20:80, while in the case of good time-managers it may be very much better. It therefore lies in our power to alter the *Pareto Time Principle*, and one of our aims must be to do just that. The *Pareto Time Principle* is only a guide to what happens if we don't take things into our own hands. Once we are aware of the lesson the *Principle* is teaching us, we can be much more realistic about whether a large proportion of the time spent on any undertaking is really producing commensurate results. Is 80 per cent of the time I'm spending on this particular task only producing 20 per cent of my results? Is the extra time spent going over and over something for the sake of one or two doubtful improvements really well spent? Is the amount of time spent thinking and discussing something before doing it really a useful contribution to the final outcome?

Suggesting that you be realistic isn't an invitation to skimp on what you are doing, simply a suggestion that you should be more perceptive about what you *are* doing. The *Pareto Time Principle* is a metaphorical nudge in the ribs, and we should take heed of it, particularly when we recognize that the low-yield 80 per cent of our time almost certainly contains periods when absolutely nothing at all is getting done.

DON'T BE TOO BUSY

There is a song I remember first hearing during a school concert when I was a boy. It still crops up regularly on children's programmes (where I hope it's message isn't lost) and starts with the lines: 'We're busy doing nothing, working the whole day through,/Trying to find lots of things not to do . . .'

It would be cynical to suggest that any of us actively try and find things not to do, but it is certainly true that we can be very busy doing nothing. By 'nothing' I mean work that is of no real value to ourselves or to anyone else. This is time-*mis*management of the highest order. Because we're so busy doing 'nothing', we have no time to look around us and see what really needs doing, no time to draw up our objectives and settle on our priorities, no time to assess why so much of what we are doing actually amounts to so very little, no time to wonder why we are stuck in the 20:80 ratio of the *Pareto Time Principle* – and no time to give ourselves any of the space we need in order to relax, recharge our batteries, incubate new ideas, look after our physical and mental health and generally watch the world go by.

However, whether our busyness is to no real purpose or to good purpose, it is good to remember the rule sometimes quoted in management training, namely that if you're too busy to relax, then you're too busy. We can only work efficiently and effectively if we give ourselves sufficient time off from work. Remember Alice and the Red Queen? Alice not only failed to get anywhere with all her running, but was rewarded only with a very dry biscuit for her pains. We are all individuals and vary in the amount of time we can regularly spend on-task. Some people have long concentration spans, others need to take frequent short breaks. Some people seem to have boundless mental and physical energy, others tire quickly. But whatever our constitution, we all need time to relax, and time to take stock of whether we really are getting somewhere with all our running, and to determine whether there are ways of ensuring we get a thirst-quenching glass of water for our efforts instead of a very dry biscuit.

Look back at the time schedule you drew up in Chapter 3. There are only so many hours in a day and so many hours in a week. One can't be categorical – let me repeat that we are all individuals – but a rough rule of thumb is that at the very least you should never for any length of time be too busy to:

- relax for one hour every evening before going to bed
  (for the benefit of your sleep);

- have one hour every day to pursue an interest or hobby
  (for the sake of your sanity);

- exercise for one half-hour at least four times a week
  (for the benefit of your health);

- take two and a half *uninterrupted* hours for meal breaks each day
  (for the benefit of your digestion).

This is a minimum of four and a half hours that should on average be free from work each weekday. This isn't much. Assuming roughly eight hours are spent in bed, this still leaves more than 11 hours (less travelling time) that you can spend each day on your work. Surely this is more than enough, especially if you manage these 11 hours sensibly?

If, nevertheless, you ignore this kind of advice and pride yourself on working every waking hour, ask yourself whether you are working primarily in order to get things done, or primarily for the sake of working. If the answer is the latter, than you could qualify for the term *workaholic*. Workaholics can be characterized as people who are unable to take proper holidays, to tolerate empty briefcases, to delegate, to stop thinking about work, or to remember the names of their children. Whether such a description is justified or not, there is no doubt that the workaholic is someone who has little or no time for anything other than work. For the workaholic, work may be a way of escaping from any number of things (ranging from an unhappy home to guilty feelings over leisure), but one thing is certain – even though this may not be the conscious intention, for the workaholic work is a way of escaping from personal life.

Of course, not everyone who works long hours is a workaholic. The term workaholic suggests a compulsive addiction to work, and the point about an addiction is that the addict cannot do without the fix concerned, however harmful it may be for his or her psychological or physical health. In this sense, the workaholic is actively persecuted by work, and may derive little actual enjoyment from the work-process itself. The hard worker by contrast (some experts suggests we should use the term *work enthusiast*) works in order to get things done, enjoys work, knows when to stop and find time for other things, and may indeed end up being significantly more productive than the workaholic. The difference between the two categories is an important one for our understanding of both the kind of stress and the kind of fulfilment that work can bring, and well worth exploring if you feel you may be slipping into the workaholic camp.

KNOW WHEN TO DO WHAT

Since the early work of Halberg and others (see Halberg, 1960), the existence of human circadian rhythms (biorhythms) is well-known to biologists and psychologists. Circadian rhythms dictate that there are certain times of the day when we are at our best both physically and psychologically. At its simplest, some of us feel most alive and creative in the mornings, while come the evenings we are fit only for collapsing with a good book or in front of the television. Others of us note that in the morning we take a great deal of time to get going physically and mentally, but by the evening are full of energy and bright ideas, while some of us (rather fewer) feel most alert and vigorous in the late afternoon.

In order to manage time effectively, note your own rhythm, and plan your day's work accordingly. A job that may take 10 minutes if tackled when you are at your best may take twice as long if tackled at the wrong time. If you are more effective at problem-solving and generating new ideas in the morning, use this time for your more creative work, and keep routine matters for the afternoon. If you feel grumpy early in the day and in a better mood after lunch, put off such things as interviews and meetings with colleagues until later in the day. If you tend to feel bored and restless around 3 p.m., use this time for tasks that get you out of the office and into the open air.

Irrespective of our personal rhythms, most of us have a productive period between 10 a.m. and noon, when the stomach, pancreas, spleen and heart all appear to be in active phases. Conversely, the majority of us experience a low period in the hour or two after lunch (a time when continentals sensibly take their siesta), as most of our energy is devoted to the process of digestion. The simple rules here are: don't waste too much prime time having a coffee break around 11 a.m. when you should be doing some of your best work, and don't make the after-lunch period even less productive by overloading your digestion. A short coffee or tea break is in fact best taken on arrival at the office, when it helps us start the day in a positive mood, rather than mid-morning when it interrupts the flow of our activities. Lunch is best taken early, when the pangs of hunger are only just making themselves felt and we are likely to eat less than if we leave it until later. An early lunch also means that we have more time in the afternoon to get back into our productive stride, and to clear away the routine jobs that we may prefer to leave until then.

On the subject of routine jobs, remember that most people find them twice as dull at home (when they are taking up their own time) as they do at work (when they are taking up the employer's time). Whatever your circadian rhythm, it is better therefore to make an effort to complete routine tasks during office hours, and to ensure that if work has to be taken home it is of the more interesting kind. In any case, if you are regularly taking routine jobs home, this suggests that something is wrong (remember the case of Marian earlier in the chapter). Either you are not managing time as you should, or you are being expected to do too much during the day. Whichever it is, remedial action is required (see Chapter 6 for how to respond if you're asked to take on too many new tasks).

START AND FINISH THE DAY POSITIVELY

I mentioned in the last section that a short coffee or tea break immediately upon arrival helps us start the day in a positive mood. The importance of such a mood can't be overestimated. If we begin our working day in a negative frame of mind, the usual result is that we lose valuable time before we get down to anything useful (and time lost early in the day puts more pressure on us in the remaining hours, which in turn prompts more negative feelings). We can't always feel enthusiastic about the day ahead. Even an author as prolific as J. B. Priestley admitted to indulging in elaborate pencil-sharpening and pipe-filling rituals at his desk each morning as an excuse for not actually getting down to work. But a positive mood pays enormous dividends in getting things done. Since you can't manufacture such a mood to order, these three effective strategies should help:

☐ Ensure that you have something pleasant, no matter how minor, to look forward to when you arrive each day at work. I mentioned a moment ago the value of taking your coffee break first thing. You can also reserve an interesting task with which to start the day's work. Even attending to your office plants can do the trick, as can tidying a bookshelf. But don't be tempted to go and chat to colleagues. Enjoyable as this is, it acts as a great thief of time, and can make starting work seem less attractive than ever.

☐ Resolve to always start work at the same time each morning, and keep to it. Whatever technique you use to help ease you into the working day, make sure you embark on the first of your actual tasks at this allotted time. You thus not only avoid losing the 10 minutes (which can so easily stretch to 15 and then 30) that can slip past unnoticed before you start to be productive, but you help to train your mind to switch itself into a working mode. We all tend to be creatures of habit, and nowhere is this more true than in our working lives.

☐ Contrive to have a clear idea of the priorities and tasks for the day ahead, so that time isn't lost while you ponder the daunting question of where to get started. One way of ensuring this is to list priorities at the end of the previous working day. Leave the list on your desk so that you know exactly where to begin.

In the same way that starting the day in a positive mood is important if you are to manage time effectively, so is finishing the day. If you end the day feeling fed up with everything and everybody around you (perhaps yourself included), you are not going to feel much enthusiasm for starting work again next morning. The best way to ensure you feel positive is to achieve all your objectives for the day so that you can feel well satisfied with the day's labours. You can help yourself further by planning the day so that at the end of the afternoon you have a short winding-down period, which you can spend on a pleasant and relatively undemanding task, rather than having to work feverishly right up until the last minute in order to get everything done.

If, in spite of all your efforts, a day really does go badly, don't waste time brooding unnecessarily over it. Tomorrow may be a good or at least a better day, but even if it isn't, you won't improve it by ruminating endlessly over all the things that went wrong today. Review what has happened, learn from the day any lessons it has to teach you, then consign it to the dustbin of history, pick up your belongings, and go home.

DON'T PUT OFF UNPLEASANT TASKS

We all tend to put off until 'later' the jobs we dislike doing. But if these jobs are unwelcome now, they're unlikely to be any less unwelcome in the future. And, in the meantime, we have at the back of our minds the nagging feeling that the jobs are still waiting to be done. Doing them *now* not only gets them out of the way, but also banishes the guilty feeling (and often replaces it with a pleasantly virtuous one).

Putting off unpleasant tasks has another disadvantage, in that it allows these tasks to pile up. Instead of being faced by one or two, we're faced by half a dozen or more, and the temptation then becomes to forget about them altogether, sometimes with disastrous consequences.

Unpleasant jobs form the one single category which does not benefit from being grouped. Despatch them as soon as they occur, and savour the satisfied feeling that this brings. There is one abiding principle always to keep in mind when faced with these jobs. It has all the qualities of a scientific law, and is unique in that it holds good at all times and under all conditions. Its very simplicity makes us all too often ignore its obvious truth. It is that *the only way to do something is to do it*. The law is worth emphasizing, because it is the secret *par excellence* of good time-management. Recognize it, accept it, and translate it into action, and more than half the battle of managing time is already won. Neglect it, and the battle isn't even properly joined. The corollary of the law is even simpler, and also deserves to be emphasized. It is that whatever it is you have to do, if possible you should *do it now*. Back this maxim up if necessary with others such as 'It won't be any easier later', and 'I'll be glad tomorrow that I did it today'.

DON'T PROCRASTINATE OVER DECISIONS

The same law applies to making decisions – the only way to make decisions is to make them. Certainly it is appropriate to defer them if they're dependent on information not yet on hand, or if it is clear that the right moment has not yet arrived. But once you have the information and the moment has come, hesitation not only wastes opportunities but also squanders time.

Remember that making decisions is rather like setting priorities. It may not be possible to make the perfect decision, but at least you can make the best one available. Work out what this is in just the same way that you set priorities. Make a list of all the possible decisions in a given situation, write down the most likely outcomes (positive and negative) against each of them, and then arrange these outcomes in order of priority. The one at the top of the list indicates the decision you ought to make.

It is sometimes said that one of the most important tasks for the good manager is to learn to play the percentage game. In the case of decisions, this means accepting that a certain percentage of decisions is going to turn out wrong (maybe one or two in ten), but that as the percentage of wrong decisions is massively outweighed by the percentage of right decisions, fear of making a wrong one should never be a reason for doing nothing. Certainly you can argue that the occasional act of indecision turns out by luck to be right, but here the percentages work in reverse. For every act of indecision that turns out to be right, a much greater percentage will turn out to be wrong.

PROACT RATHER THAN REACT

Still on the same theme, *pro*action is eminently preferable to *re*action. To proact (or to act) means to anticipate events and be in a position to take appropriate action as soon as the right moment arrives. To react, on the other hand, means to have little anticipation and do something only when you are overtaken by events. Proactors tend to be the people who are always one jump ahead of the field, who always seem to be in the right place at the right time, and who are always better informed than anyone else. Many of us like an easy life, and so we tend to be reactors. This means that, ostrich-like, we aren't alert to the challenges and opportunities just appearing over the horizon, with the consequence that challenges unseat us or opportunities pass us by before we're even properly aware they're upon us.

It isn't that good proactors are always looking for trouble where none exists. That way neurosis lies. It is that good proactors are able to appraise situations realistically. They know that however much we may wish it were otherwise, nothing ever stays the same. To be alive is to be surrounded by a process of change, growth, decay and regrowth. To operate successfully within this process, we have to be prepared to change along with it, and the more we can take this change into our own hands instead of waiting for it to be forced upon us, the more successful we are likely to be.

Train yourself in proaction by regularly taking the time to sit down and appraise the likely immediate future, just as you sit down and review the immediate past. Draw up a list of the developments and crises that could be lying in wait on the road ahead, then give each one a likely rating from 1 to 5, and identify the effect that those with the higher ratings might have upon you and your colleagues. Finally, note down the warning signs that will indicate if they are pending, and sketch out the action that you can best take should they actually come to pass.

MORE ABOUT PROCRASTINATION

Whether our procrastination is caused by perfectionism, as suggested earlier (we can't start on a task until we know we are going to get it right), insecurity (we're sure before we start that we are going to get it wrong), or genuine indecision over the issues involved, there are a number of techniques that can help us.

The so called *salami* (or *slice-up*) technique suggests that, where possible, a big decision should be broken down into several smaller ones, and each one tackled in turn.

The *balance-sheet* technique suggests you should set out all the pros and cons (see also page 72), and make your decision on the strength of them (this method is also helpful in ensuring you get together all the information you need upon which to base the decision).

The *procrastination drawer* technique suggests you put every-thing connected with a difficult decision into a drawer and leave them there until the need for the decision has gone away, then pull them out and announce you are 'working on it' if anyone enquires (not to be recommended!).

The *reward* technique suggests you identify a really big reward for yourself which you can only have when the decision has been sensibly and fully taken.

The *committee* technique suggests you hand everything over to other people and let them decide. ('Let's be democratic about this').

The first two techniques plus the reward technique are the ones which good time-managers should use.

TAKE THE BLAME FOR YOUR OWN TIME LOSSES

Psychologists recognize that we differ in the way in which we characteristically attribute responsibility for the various things that happen to us in life (Weiner, 1979). One of the ways in which we do this is known as *locus of control*. At its simplest, some individuals have a predominantly *external* locus of control, and attribute responsibility to outside causes (for example, the faults of others or the help given by them, the force of circumstances, the activities of Lady Luck) while with other individuals the locus of control is predominantly *internal*, and responsibility is attributed to oneself (for example, one's own abilities, or hard work, or lack of them).

However the picture usually isn't as simple as this. Many people's locus of control is more likely to be situation-specific, for example internal in certain areas, such as their social lives, and external in others, such as their working lives. Or, to take another example, they may attribute certain kinds of results to themselves, for example, their successes, and certain kinds of results to other people, for example, their failures. Obviously the best kind of locus of control is one that is realistic and able to attribute every effect to its appropriate cause, and this is particularly important when it comes to time-management. Certainly there are occasions when other people are more responsible for our time loss than we are, but for most of us, and for most of the time, the blame must fall fairly and squarely upon ourselves.

Since we may have got into the habit of ignoring this fact, it is helpful to look at the language we use when we recognize time loss, and change it so that it more accurately reflects our *own* responsibility for this loss. It is also helpful to look at the way in which, even when we do take responsibility for our use of time, we employ euphemistic language instead of really facing up to what it is we are doing. Let's take some common examples of this language misuse and suggest how the statements could be changed to reflect more accurately what is really happening:

'Where has the time gone?'	*change to*	'How did I use the time?'
'It was such a waste of time'	*change to*	'I wasted so much time'
'The time just flew past'	*change to*	'I didn't keep proper track of time'

'The time went nowhere'	*change to*	'I didn't make best use of time'
'It (or they) took up so much of my time'	*change to*	'I let it (or them) take up so much of my time'
'Where has the day gone?'	*change to*	'What have I done with the day?'
'It's a way of killing time	*change to*	'It's a way of squandering time'
'It's a pleasant pastime'	*change to*	'It's pleasant but unproductive'

Using more accurate language in this way doesn't mean we should always be hyperconscious of time passing, but it does mean we should be more aware of the need to reflect whether it was well spent or not. If we decide it was, fine. If we decide it wasn't, then provided we're serious about good time-management we need to give thought as to whether time should be spent in similar ways in the future.

USE YOUR MEMORY MORE EFFECTIVELY

The human memory is a strange thing. It often seems to clutter itself up with trivia that is of no obvious value to us, and with experiences that we would much rather forget, while it stubbornly refuses to retain the things that we really want to retain. But our memories are actually very much better than we imagine. If I asked you to sit down and write all you know (the single question reputedly used in certain imperial service examinations in ancient China) you would still be scribbling away industriously this time tomorrow, and probably way beyond that. Our memories are vastly effective storehouses of hundreds upon hundreds of facts, ideas, experiences, sensations, and even moods. The main reason why we are often unable to recall the things we want to recall at the times when we want to recall them is that we put the blame for our failures on the poor quality of an impersonal-sounding organ called our 'memory' instead of upon our own poor use of it.

The result is that we effectively cease to take responsibility for our own forgetting, and we make no effort to improve matters, rather as if our memories are fixed like the size of our brains, or our height, or the size of our ears. The truth of the matter is that, with only a little effort, we can become much more effective at using our memory powers, with all the bonus that this brings for our management of time. There are a number of good books available on the memory and its proper use (for example Brown, 1979; Klatzky, 1980; Baddeley, 1983), but the main techniques for memory improvement are neither difficult to explain nor difficult to learn. I'll summarize the most helpful of them:

BE MINDFUL

It's a fact of life that much of the time we forget things simply because we haven't paid proper attention to them in the first place. This is particularly true of those small, but maddening and time-wasting, examples of memory failure that assail us so frequently during the working day. We put something down, and a moment later can't remember where we put it, and have to spend precious minutes hunting for it. I discussed in Chapter 4 the importance of keeping a record of where we put short-stay items, but I'm talking now about those even shorter-stay items – a pen, a letter we were in the middle of reading when the phone went and which we put down somewhere, the notes we've just made of an interview and which were here a minute ago, the important document we took out of the file and which has now mysteriously vanished.

The problem is that when we put these things down our minds were on something else. We were not concentrating upon what we were doing, so it isn't surprising that we can't remember what it is we've just done. The remedy is simple. Concentrate. Be mindful: keep your mind in the present moment, instead of woolgathering about other matters in the future or in the past. Since this is difficult to do without a little practice, help yourself by setting up a silent running commentary during those moments when you are switching from one activity to another, or when you are trying to do 101 things at once. This technique sometimes amuses people when I explain it to them at workshops, but they soon discover how effective it is, and how easy it is to do. After all, you're thinking about *something* virtually every moment of your waking life. All the running commentary does is to ensure that you are actually thinking about what it is you are doing – in other words that it is on your job and not somewhere else. If you think such a running commentary is boring, think how much more boring it is looking for the items you've mislaid.

BE A BETTER LISTENER

In the same way that, much of the time, we're not paying attention to what it is we're doing, much of the time we're not paying attention to what it is people are saying. We are poor listeners. For present purposes I am not referring to the listening skills of the good counsellor or the good physician, simply to the skills needed to register properly the bits of information that people are constantly firing at us (see Nelson-Jones, 1986; Fontana, 1990). Discipline yourself to stop your own train of thought when others are talking to you, and register clearly whatever it is they are trying to say. If you haven't heard it properly, ask for it to be repeated, more than once if need be. Repetition has the advantage of ensuring you've heard correctly in the first place, and also allows time for the information concerned to be transferred from your short-term to your long-term memory. All incoming information is held first in short-term memory, and a pause is usually required if it is to be transferred effectively to long-term. Notice how the telephone number you've just looked up stays in your mind for the brief moment required for dialling, then vanishes without trace. If you wished to retain it, you would have to repeat it to yourself (or hold it visually in your mind or associate it with a number you already know, or process it in some other way) in order for transfer to long-term memory to take place.

USE ASSOCIATIONS

Much time is lost through difficulties in remembering isolated facts, particularly the names of people you have never met, or abstractions like dates or lists of numbers. The secret here is to end their isolation by always trying to associate them with something that is already familiar to you. Recalling things that have these familiar associations is always easier than recalling things that do not. And if a particular name or number has no association, then invent one for it, the more unusual (even bizarre), the better. Let's take an example using names. If the name is one that carries an obvious meaning, such as Hill, or Green, or Turner, or Locke, or Rivers, there's no real problem. Think up a sentence containing the name and associate it with the context in which the name has to be remembered, allowing the sentence at the same time to set up a visual image if possible in your mind. 'This letter from Mrs Hill must have come uphill to get here', 'I have to call on Mr Green; I wonder if he'll turn green when he sees me', 'Miss Turner has asked me to turn up and speak to her students'. If the name has no meaning, think of a word or phrase that sound like it and that does have meaning, and use that instead. Thus 'Brent' would become 'bent', and be incorporated into a sentence like 'Mr Brent bent over backwards to be helpful', 'Cortell' become 'cor-tell' and gives rise to a sentence like 'Cor, I'll tell Mr Cortell a thing or two when I see him tomorrow' and so on.

Dates and lists of numbers can best be remembered by associating each number up to '9' (plus '0') with an object it resembles and which in itself is easily remembered. Thus for example; '1' could become a candle, '2' a swan, '3' a trident, '4' an axe, '5' a hand, '6' a pipe, '7' an old-fashioned razor, '8' a pair of spectacles, '9' a wineglass, and '0' an orange. Now when you have to remember a date or a string of numbers, make up a sentence incorporating the objects associated with the digits concerned, again visualizing them if you can. Thus if you wanted to remember the date on which the Second World War ended, 1945, this might become 'The war ended when I put the *candle* in the *wineglass* in order to take the *axe* in my *hand*'. I have sometimes been asked by students or in workshops whether it isn't easier just to remember the numbers, rather than a whole sentence. My answer is, 'Let's try it and see'. After dividing those present into two groups, and giving each group a string of dates to remember, one with the help of this method and one without, it can rapidly become clear to everyone that it most definitely is not.

ORGANIZE INCOMING INFORMATION

Imagine you are sitting in a room and receiving goods for a jumble sale. People arrive from time to time and hand you various different things. What do you do with them? Naturally enough, you sort as many of them as possible as they are handed to you, putting them into different piles. This will allow you to see at a glance what you've got, and to find things for people as soon as you are asked. By organizing the things as soon as you are given them, you make your job of coping with them later very much easier.

It's the same with memory. If we can organize the different pieces of information that are given to us during the day, we stand a much better chance of retaining them and of recalling them readily as the need arises. There are various different ways of carrying out this task of mental organization, but none of them is likely to be successful unless you work it out carefully beforehand and spend a little time practising it.

This means the creation of a mental filing system, so that as each piece of information arrives it can be consciously assigned to its correct category. Much of the most important information with which we have to deal comes to us verbally, from colleagues as well as from clients. If it were always possible to ask that the information be put in writing, or if it were always possible to make written notes of it, everything would be fine. But frequently neither of these things is realistic, and a mental filing system thus becomes essential. How is this system best organized? This is up to the ingenuity of the individual, since you need to discover what works best for you. But many people find a simple *colour* system operates well. The most effective way is to use the colours red, yellow, blue and green as follows:

red – very important/urgent pieces of information

yellow – less important/urgent but still relevant pieces of information

blue – interesting longer-term issues

green – peripheral but potentially relevant matters

Anything that does not qualify for one of these files is mentally dumped as soon as it is received. Each time an item of relevant information arrives verbally, it is mentally placed in the relevant file, and visualized as written there in the colour concerned. As soon as possible afterwards, the file is mentally 'opened', the piece of information recalled, and either dealt with or actually written down.

LOOK FOR STRUCTURE

If you try to memorize the numbers from 1 to 100 in random sequence the task becomes almost impossible. But if you organize them into their correct order, you simply have to remember four units of information, namely the words 'numbers 1 to 100'. Rearranged into their correct order, the numbers possess a structure, and the recall of this structure is much easier than the recall of random pieces of information. In all memory tasks, much time is saved by identifying any structure that happens to be present. Structure is essentially the meaningful pattern or patterns underlying information. Sometimes it carries a logical form, as in the case of the numbers 1 to 100. At other times it depends primarily upon a common set of properties such as those which allow us to place information into categories.

Structure may also be a much looser affair, and depend only upon associations, in the way that we associate certain actions with certain people, or associate certain headaches with certain tasks. But whatever the structure involved, relate incoming information wherever possible to some aspect of it. Thus each new fact, statistic or technique is linked to what is already known in much the same way that individual pieces are fitted into a jigsaw.

Try also to look for the structure or for the substance behind what people are saying, and be bold enough to ask for relevant details if you can't recognize them at first sight ('Are you saying that . . .?', 'Am I right in thinking you mean . . .?', 'Is your argument that . . .?) and committing this structure to memory, provided you decide it is worth it. In your own work, aim at being equally direct and to the point. Say or write what needs to be said or written, and don't waste your own and other people's time on unnecessary obfuscation. And resolve *never* to become one of those individuals who steal the time of others by taking 10 minutes to say what could be better said in one.

AIM FOR EXCELLENCE RATHER THAN PERFECTION

In professional life, perfectionism can be a major source of stress. It can also be one of the major causes of time loss. It's right and proper to want to carry out tasks to the best of one's abilities, but perfectionism (as I mentioned earlier in this chapter) can suggest an insecurity which leads to an obsessive or near-obsessive concern with getting things just right. I also mentioned earlier that this insecurity may lead to many things being left unfinished, and in the case of the perfectionist many things that are not even started, since he or she knows so much effort will have to go into revising and re-revising minor details that even the smallest task can seem impossibly daunting in prospect. Far from being a means towards better results, perfectionism can thus sometimes be a means towards no results at all. Hardly surprisingly, it is sometimes said that the price of perfectionism is prohibitively high.

The solution is to replace perfectionism with excellence. Excellence is not only achievable, it can also, paradoxically, often approach perfection closer than perfectionism itself. Frequently the writer, for example, can find that numerous attempts to rewrite a particular sentence produce a final version which, on inspection, turns out to be inferior to an earlier attempt rejected over an hour ago. The manager or the social worker may find that an initial, realistic solution to a problem is more effective than an over-elaborated one conceived after lengthy debate and reflection. Perfectionism is often counterproductive, and can lead one to spend so long in the fruitless quest for ideal results that both time and creativity are squandered. There is a need to revise and rethink ideas, and to criticize and edit one's work, but it is tragic if the critic and the editor in us end up by killing the poor author.

People in professional life can have a strong streak of perfection-ism in them without realizing it is there. Check whether you are one of them by:

• recording how long particular tasks take you, and then analysing how much of that time was spent on what I call 'authoring' (that is, actually doing or producing), and how much was spent 'editing' (criticizing, debating, rejecting). If more time is consistently spent upon 'editing' than upon 'authoring', you should look seriously at whether you are aiming for perfection rather than excellence;

• asking yourself each time you fail to finish a task the *real* reason for non-completion. Has it, for example, anything to do with fears that the finished product will not be good enough?

• identifying *why* particular tasks may seem daunting in prospect; is it because of *task-demands* or because of *self-demands*?

If you do detect extremes of perfectionism in yourself, look to see whether insecurity is the cause. Insecurity is characterized by fear – in this case either fear of the judgement of others or of self-judgement. Help yourself overcome this fear by drawing up objectives for each task and focusing upon *essentials* (including the simple facts of starting and finishing). If the task has to do with writing reports or letters, or drawing up lists of recommendations, resolve to come to the end of the task (that way you'll work quicker and at least be assured of a first draft) before you start revising, rather than endlessly revising and re-revising as you go along. If the tasks are more practical ones, allow yourself to brainstorm ideas when first facing them, generating as many ideas as possible in connection with them without censoring these ideas, and only weigh up their relative merits when your creativity comes to a stop. Commit these ideas to paper or to tape. Even the least promising of them could turn out to be a stroke of genius when you come to develop it. Never frustrate your own productivity, and don't be too hard on yourself when you do finally come to criticize and edit your ideas or your efforts. Accept that the fundamental requirements of any task have far more to do with building up than with tearing down, and that to be hypercritical is the surest way of achieving only the latter. An abandoned task that aimed at perfection compares poorly with a finished task that achieves excellence.

DON'T CONFUSE EFFICIENCY WITH EFFECTIVENESS

We can be highly efficient at doing a highly unproductive job. *Efficiency* simply means that whatever we happen to be doing, we are doing it in a well-organized and time-saving way. This is fine if what we are doing is worth doing. And this is where effectiveness comes in. *Effectiveness* has to do with setting productive objectives and achieving them. Simply because you are efficient doesn't mean you are effective, and major problems arise if the two things are confused. *Effectiveness* comes first, and *efficiency* should be used as its servant. Throughout this book the emphasis is upon this order. Beware of efficiency on its own.

FRIEND OR ENEMY?

When it comes to time-management you are potentially your own best friend – or your own worst enemy. The choice is largely in your own hands. Psychology is essentially a way of learning about yourself, not just about other people, and the psychology of time-management is concerned with learning to use yourself to best advantage. Even when you're at work there is no such thing as your own time and your employer's time. It's all 'your' time, and so it's up to you how productive or otherwise it turns out to be. Study yourself and see how you can get the best out of yourself. There is a sense – and this is not being fanciful – in which each of us *is* time, because every one of our actions and our thoughts takes place in time and not outside it. Time isn't something 'out there', an objective something going on distinct and separate from us. Time is the stuff of our lives, so to study how we are using it is also to study how our lives are being lived.

Chapter Six

You and Others

At the end of the previous chapter, I emphasized that you can be your own best friend or your own worst enemy when it comes to managing time. This means that although other people can save time for you or waste it, it's mainly up to you which they do. Of course, it hardly needs saying that the value of social relationships doesn't rest solely upon whether others gain or lose time for us. Social relationships provide us with friendship, emotional and professional support, amusement, and all the other things upon which much of our psychological well-being depends. But notice how welcome even a casual acquaintance is if he or she sees you need help and gives it promptly and effectively, and how even the best of friends can be less welcome than usual if they drop in for a leisurely social chat just when you're desperate to finish an urgent task. A conflict is at once set up between your pleasure in their company and your anxiety over your work, and even if pleasure wins out over anxiety, you are unlikely to be at your social best in these circumstances.

A similar conflict can be set up with clients. However much we want to give them our professional support, if they hold us up unnecessarily on a busy day or come at the wrong time it's hard to feel that all is sweetness and light. When we're up to our eyes in work, the clients who most gain our gratitude are those who say what needs to be said clearly and directly, and then leave us to get on with things, or the ones who see we're busy and volunteer to come back later.

However, some people, colleagues and clients alike, are notoriously insensitive to our social needs. By temperament, or by inexperience, they fail to recognize the signals that say we want help or that we're busy. And there are always those who recognize the signals but for their own purposes chose to ignore them. In order to ensure that others allow us to make best use of our time in professional life we therefore have to develop two important skills:

☐ Firstly, we have to know how to ask (and *who* to ask) for help when it's needed (this includes knowing where to go for information or guidance).

☐ Secondly, we have to be able to indicate, without giving unnecessary offence, that we're too busy at the moment to deal with a particular issue or to engage in social chitchat, however pleasant.

I will examine these two skills in turn.

HOW TO ASK FOR HELP

DELEGATING

How to ask for help raises first and foremost the question of how to delegate, for delegation is essentially a way of obtaining help. Even though you may have a right to delegate to others by virtue of your position, delegation is by no means as straightforward as it may seem, since it always carries with it an element of risk by the very fact that you are assigning to someone else work for which you carry the prime responsibility. You hope they will undertake it sufficiently well to both save you time and protect you from the recriminations that would arise from mistakes, but this hope may go unfulfilled. Other people don't always do what you are convinced you asked them to do, and after a few unhappy experiences many of us may prefer not to delegate, and may continue to carry the whole burden on our own shoulders. Effective delegation does not therefore come easily, and there is no doubt that it is an important skill in its own right, carrying with it a number of specific requirements. The first of these – and one frequently overlooked even by specialist books on the subject – consists of the ability to recognize when delegation is *really needed*.

RECOGNIZING THE NEED FOR DELEGATION
It is sometimes hard to accept that we stand in need of the help that delegation can bring, and there are several possible reasons for this.

● We may feel that to ask for help is a sign of weakness.

- We may believe we are indispensable and no one else will do the job as well as we can.

- We may be afraid someone else will do the job better than we can and take the credit.

- We may feel there is no one who can help anyway.

- We may feel guilty at delegating, or may enjoy all aspects of our work so much that we are reluctant to let anything go.

The first of these reasons can stem from a similar psychological cause to that discussed under perfectionism earlier, namely insecurity. We may feel that any hint of weakness diminishes us in the eyes of others and of ourselves, and this prevents us from identifying when it is legitimate to ask for help. It also prevents us from recognizing that it is a sign of strength to know and accept our own limitations, and a sign of weakness to pretend to ourselves and others that such limitations don't exist.

The second reason is also bound up with our feelings of self-worth. To be thought indispensable is a tremendous boost to the ego. The trouble is that it is a false boost. History shows us that there have been very few truly indispensable individuals and that it is more valuable to aim at being a good leader than to aim at being an indispensable one. One of the prime qualities of good leaders is that they develop the abilities of those around them so that there is always someone capable of deputizing when the need arises. If, in spite of this, our ego still demands we think of ourselves as indispensable, we must recognize there is something particularly fragile about it, and something that is in for a body blow when age finally dictates that the time has come to step down from office whether we like it or not.

The third reason needs little comment. If we're jealous of the success of those responsible to us, and want all the credit for ourselves, then we have to do some thinking about the causes of this jealousy and about our attitude towards the people who have to work for us.

The fourth reason – a feeling that there is no one else to help us anyway – is another sign of poor leadership. The good leader is one who can recognize and develop the gifts of others, no matter how rudimentary these gifts are initially. If there is no one to whom we can look for help in the days when we need it, this is usually a sign that we didn't do enough to train and prepare others in the days when we didn't need help.

The fifth reason may relate back to what was said respectively about the workaholic and the work enthusiast on page 68. If you feel guilty at delegating (assuming there are no valid reasons for this such as work-overload on the part of the subordinate concerned) then the answer is that you must be more realistic in your self-expectations. If you drive yourself into the ground, in the end everything will have to be delegated, as you simply won't be around to do any of your work. If by contrast you enjoy your work too much to let any of it go, you have to remind yourself that others might just enjoy it too. Unwittingly, there is the danger of keeping to ourselves things which should rightly be shared with others.

Even if you feel none of these reasons for being a poor delegator apply, you may still not be making full use of your powers of delegation, or may be delegating inappropriately. *Exercise 8* (page 88) may help to clarify things further. Some of the questions may not apply to your own work circumstances, in which case you can ignore them.

If after self-examination you still find it hard to delegate, remember that delegation is not only of benefit to you. Those working under you need the experience and responsibility that delegation brings. It is highly frustrating to work for someone who insists on keeping all the reigns of power in his or her own hands. And frustration does not bring out the best in people, with the result that they may perform badly even on those low-grade tasks which we are prepared to entrust to them – with the consequence that we have to waste time supervising these tasks when we would be far better employed doing more important things.

WHAT TO DELEGATE

Once having recognized that delegation is called for, the next question is what to delegate. In many professional or business hierarchies there are job specifications which indicate who should do what, but they usually cover only the broad generalities rather than specific details. The majority of the decisions as to who does what may therefore still be left to those actually in charge. In taking these decisions, there are some important considerations to keep in mind.

☐ Don't trap yourself into delegating only the jobs that others can do *better or as well as you*. The prime purpose of delegation is to free you to do jobs that others at present can't be asked to do.

CAN YOU DELEGATE?

EXERCISE 8

Yes No

1. Do you insist on seeing and signing all the letters that leave your department?

2. Do you insist on making all the important financial decisions?

3. Are there usually a substantial number of unsolved problems and unmade decisions awaiting you when you have been away for any length of time?

4. Do you consider it important to know the exact workload of each person working under you?

5. Do you frequently find yourself rejecting or changing decisions made by those to whom you delegated tasks?

6. Are you usually the last person to leave the office at night?

7. Are you impatient of the shortcomings of those working under you?

8. Do you often delegate tasks to people which they are forced to do in the evenings or over weekends?

9. Do you feel the need to keep tabs on everything that goes on in your department or office?

10. Do you insist that delegated tasks must normally take precedence over a subordinate's other work?

A 'yes' response to any of these questions suggests you may need to work on improving your delegation skills in at least some areas. If you have answered 'yes' to half or more of the questions attempted, this suggests that working on improving these skills could be a matter of some urgency.

Many delegated jobs may not be done as well as you would do them, but that isn't a reason for refusing to delegate.

☐ Don't delegate only the unpleasant jobs. If you are to bring out the best in the people working for you they must be given their share of the smooth as well as of the rough.

☐ On the other hand, don't keep all the unpleasant jobs for yourself in the mistaken belief you can't ask others to do things you yourself dislike. This is both unfair to you and poor training for them. They have to learn to be successful at all kinds of jobs.

☐ Don't delegate unfairly. People rarely work well if they feel they have been given an unwelcome task that clearly belongs to another colleague (or worse still belongs to you). They also rarely feel happy if a welcome task that clearly belongs to them goes to someone else.

BE SPECIFIC

When planning how you are going to delegate, it pays to be specific. It is of limited value to enter against a particular objective 'Delegate this to John'. Instead, specify exactly what you expect John to do, and the precise time-frame within which you expect him to do it. Thus you might write in your plan:

> Instruct John to prepare a report (circa 3,000 words) by January 31st to help me take decisions on updating or replacing departmental IT equipment. The report must detail:
> a) the working capabilities of our existing equipement;
> b) the areas of malfunction or obsolescence;
> c) the approximate cost of repairs and/or replacements;
> d) the details of relevant contractors and/or suppliers;
> e) the time-frame contractors/suppliers would need in order to meet our various possible requirements.

Note that this plan follows the five rules of delegation in that it makes clear *what* has to be done, *why* it has to be done, *how* it has to be done, *who* has to do it, and by *when* it has to be done.

At the bottom of the plan, make clear also when this task is to be given to John. It is no good delegating it to him at the last minute, when you have finally decided you can't possibly do everything yourself. Delegating it at the last minute is unfair to John, and probably means that he won't be able to do the job properly, and you will end up having to do most of it yourself after all.

If you're fortunate enough to have someone who is specifically there to stand in for you, good time-management demands you give them clear areas of responsibility, so that they are not constantly forced to refer unnecessary matters to you. Their areas of responsibility should invariably be put in writing, signed by both you and your deputy, and copies held by the pair of you. Regularly review these areas in the light of the experience of both of you, and amend, delete, or add to them as required.

Once jobs have been delegated, allow people a reasonable amount of freedom to get on and do them. You will not be managing your own time or theirs effectively if you are constantly asking them to report back to you or unnecessarily supervising or interfering with what they are doing. If you have picked the right people for the job, they should be allowed to get on with it. Ensure however that you give them:

- a clear brief at the outset as to what the job entails;

- guidance on when they need refer back to you and when they need not;

- opportunities to use initiative wherever appropriate – don't structure the job so tightly for them that they have no room to manoeuvre;

- your support when they require it;

- the knowledge that they need not be afraid to confess mistakes to you (especially as the longer these mistakes remain hidden, the more time you may lose correcting them when they do eventually come to light);

- praise and recognition for a job well done.

Don't forget that there is such a thing as *upward delegation*. In practical terms, this means not wasting time on a task that clearly should be referred to your superior. Be sure that when you do refer it on however, you provide along with it any information and/or recommendations that may be helpful. This saves time for your superior, saves time for you (they would probably only ask you to put the information together anyway) and also serves as confirmation of your own efficiency.

There is also such a thing as *sideways delegation*, which means passing over to colleagues the things that clearly lie in their areas of responsibility. In order to do this successfully, make sure you have

WHAT SORT OF TASKS SHOULD BE DELEGATED?

This is up to you, in the sense that only you know the full situation and the interests and abilities of those working with you. But the standard *general* guidance given on what to delegate (Reynolds and Tramel, 1985; Seiwert, 1991) suggests you should give particular thought to:

fact-finding tasks;

first drafts of written material (such as reports, letters, information sheets);

problem analysis and suggested solutions;

data collection;

one-off tasks;

training tasks (tasks that provide subordinates with necessary experience or which allow them to provide training for others);

routine tasks;

feasibility tasks (tasks exploring possibilities in new areas);

follow-up tasks (tasks connected with projects that have already been established and which are now running well);

clear-up and completion tasks (tasks involving the straightforward conclusion of projects that have run their course);

summaries of important but lengthy incoming material;

communication and opinion-sounding tasks (tasks involving contacting a list of colleagues to give information or collect views); and

interim and progress reports.

an accurate idea of who is supposed to do what in your department or office. If some areas of responsibility are unclear, list them and bring the matter forward to the next departmental meeting. Even where things are clearcut, a friendly accompanying note to the colleague concerned (who may already feel overworked) helps him or her feel appreciated, and can avoid unnecessary attempts to re-delegate the work back to you.

Finally, tasks can be delegated to a specially formed working party, or put on the agenda of a committee. If a working party is involved, then the guidelines for delegation to individuals (page 87) all apply. But both working parties and the deliberations of committees take up a great deal of people's time, and a useful rule in all delegation strategies is that one should never involve more people in any task than is really necessary. Even highly efficient people can get in each other's way unless there is a clear need for all their services and a clear division of labour between them.

KNOWING WHERE TO GO FOR INFORMATION OR GUIDANCE

We can't carry everything in our heads, and there are frequently times when we need information or guidance from others. The good time-manager knows where to go for this information and guidance, and how best to ask for it. For example, when we're chasing information we often find an inordinate amount of time is wasted while we are passed from one person to another (frequently while on the telephone) until we find someone in a position to give the required help. During this process we have to repeat our story to each person, a frustrating business that can leave us tempted to cut our losses and abandon the whole exercise. Much of this time-wasting can be avoided if we keep careful records of the various people and agencies who have helped us in the past, noting against each the kind of problem with which their help was given. It is worth keeping an indexed notebook specially for this purpose, and methodically filling it in whenever appropri-ate (it's surprising how quickly the information builds up). This allows you to ask for someone *by name* when you're looking for help, an essential strategy when dealing with large organizations.

If you don't have a specific name, anticipate that you're about to embark on the game of pass-the-person with yourself as victim, and prepare in advance a brief and accurate statement of your needs so that this can be briskly repeated each time you're passed on, and the person at the other end (who in all probability also wants to manage time) allowed quickly to grasp what it is you require. And when announcing these needs, 'I want to speak to the person responsible for . . .' is a better opening statement than 'I'd like to speak to someone who can help me with . . .', since the latter suggests you have no real right to ask and risks a dismissive response.

It is also advisable to allocate a block of time, as the occasion arises, specifically for information seeking. Make a list of the most frequently occurring topics on which information is needed, and go down the list asking against each item, 'Where can I go for this?' With the help of a few telephone calls you can build up a most useful data bank which can be entered into your indexed notebook or onto your computer.

COMMUNICATING WITH COLLEAGUES

AREAS OF RESPONSIBILITY

It is valuable to know exactly to whom you are responsible for each area of your own work. In professional life we are often very lax about this, and are then surprised when a crisis arises and someone blames us for not keeping them informed of issues we didn't realize lay in their jurisdiction, or conversely denies responsibility for issues we believed most certainly did. Analyse each aspect of your job regularly and make sure you know to whom you should report or liaise with in connection with it. Ensure that wherever possible you get important instructions in writing (and file them properly). If others are reluctant to commit themselves to paper (some people are notorious for this), write the instructions down yourself as you understand them, and send a letter asking to be informed in writing whether you are correct or not. If the person concerned fails to reply, send them another copy of your letter, and then a further follow-up copy. Keep a record of the dates on which these copies were sent. People can all too readily say they never received your original letter, but they can hardly stick to this story after you've bombarded them with two additional copies. If you still receive no reply, write again indicating that as you have had no response you assume that the situation is as set out in your first letter. Again send two copies.

This may sound like time-consumption instead of time-management, but it's a much quicker process than having to deal with all the arguments, accusations and counter-accusations consequent upon making mistakes. Provided you know your own position is clear, you simply have to state it (together with supporting documentation), should mistakes occur, and cut short interminable post-mortem wranglings.

Making the position clear at the outset in this way also means that you don't have to waste time constantly going back for clarification on each individual point of obscurity. Don't, by the way, be tempted to use the phone as a substitute for the written word on these occasions. People can often deny what they said to you over the phone, or with the best will in the world their meaning may be ambiguous, or you may unwittingly misinterpret what it is they tried to tell you. Having something in writing gives you a permanent record, and allows you to identify and rectify any areas of possible confusion long before mistakes are given the chance to occur.

COMMUNICATING EFFECTIVELY

The preceding points relate to the important business of communicating effectively with colleagues, and in this context there are a number of other considerations to keep in mind. A great deal of time is lost at all levels of professional life because channels of communication break down or are nonexistent in the first place. Even more is lost because many people communicate far too much unnecessary information, so that what is important becomes buried in a welter of overwritten or irrelevant nonsense.

We can break down the subject of communication into two parts, *incoming communications* and *outgoing communications*, and look at these separately.

INCOMING COMMUNICATIONS
If you work in a large department, the first step is to ensure that there are proper communication channels operating. Nobody (except those with vested interests in keeping others in ignorance) enjoys poor communication within an organization, and if it is clear things need to be improved, put an item to that effect on the agenda of the next relevant meeting. Get the support of colleagues in advance, and circulate some *brief* suggestions on how the communications machinery can be improved. Avoid cumbersome proposals that will take more time to implement than they will actually save. Suggest only realistic and concrete ways forward.

Supplement this by sending people a list of the things you need to know whenever you feel you are not being properly informed. General appeals such as 'Could I please be kept better informed?' are of no use. Set out succinctly in your list exactly what information you want, leaving spaces under each question for the other person to write the answers. If you receive no reply, promptly send out a duplicate copy (marking it 'duplicate copy' and 'urgent'). If appropriate, send copies 'for information' to any other people who may be involved. The thought that several people are going to become aware of his or her inefficiency is usually a powerful spur to your respondent to get on with things and give you the information you want.

The second step in improving incoming communications is to cut down on the time you spend reading unnecessary material. The standard question to ask yourself when beginning reading something you've just received is, 'What do I need to learn from this?' With a few exceptions, we usually have a good idea of the subject matter of incoming documents (reading the last paragraph first is often a help). Put this question to yourself, and keep it firmly in mind as you read the document. This allows you to skip over irrelevant paragraphs. Highlight the important bits, and put a line through all the rest.

If the incoming information is given to you verbally rather than in writing, keep the same question in mind. Most of us are too polite to try and hurry a colleague who takes twice as long to tell us something as is necessary. But this can be done without giving offence by putting questions to them designed to get at the things you really want to know (for example, 'Yes I see, but tell me whether . . .?' and so on). Supplement this by breaking in and summarizing frequently ('So what you're saying is . . .'). Speak briskly yourself, and if appropriate make brief notes of the conversation ('Let me make sure I've got this right – you've just told me that . . .').

OUTGOING COMMUNICATIONS
Take your own medicine and keep these brief and to the point, always bearing in mind the question 'What does the other person really need to know?' If you're communicating in writing, *use frequent subheadings*. This helps focus your mind and assists the reader in grasping quickly what you are saying. If you are giving information verbally, make sure the other person has been listening to what you are saying. If in doubt, don't be afraid to ask

'Have I been making that clear?'. Recognize also that some people are much more difficult to communicate with than others, and that they can waste your time by such practices as refusing to accept what you want to tell them until you've told them ten times over, or by drawing you into unnecessary arguments. Typically, such people tend to be:

suspicious individuals who doubt your every word (which can be a sign of projection – since they themselves are dishonest they automatically suspect others of dishonesty too);

authoritarian individuals who try to make you feel incompetent and foolish no matter what you're trying to say;

hostile and argumentative individuals who challenge your every word just for the sake of it;

interrupters and impatient individuals who are never prepared to hear you out.

The best general advice that can be offered (Nelson-Jones, 1986; Fontana, 1990) is to be aware of these personality characteristics in people, and refuse to allow them to succeed in making you feel inferior or in making you argue or unduly hurry what it is you are trying to say. Stick calmly to your brief. If necessary (but without being confrontational) remind them of their own behaviour ('You seem very suspicious about this for some reason'; 'You're not allowing me to present my case'; 'You seem to want to argue, but I'm much more interested in giving you the facts'; 'If you keep interrupting I'll never finish'). The difficult colleagues of this world usually feed on the fact that others are more polite, tactful and sensitive than they are. Remember that you have a right to be who you are and to say what you're saying.

INDICATING YOU'RE TOO BUSY

The best-respected people in professional life tend to be those who always seem to have time for others. But having time for others doesn't necessarily mean having time for them now, right this very minute. The secret of these well-organized folk is that they are able to sum up quickly the kind of time demands someone is going to make of them, and if these are likely to exceed the time available they make a future appointment rather than try to fit him or her into the urgency of the moment and do justice neither to them nor to the other tasks on hand. The techniques they use vary dependent upon whether they are dealing with colleagues (and friends) or with clients.

DEALING WITH COLLEAGUES AND FRIENDS

There are two extreme ways of dealing with those colleagues and friends who have a habit of dropping in and taking up your time. The first is to be so rigid in your routine that they know you never like to be disturbed during certain set periods each day. The second is to be so totally unpredictable in your habits that no one has any idea when you are likely to be found. Neither of these extremes is particularly to be recommended, though if you find you work best with a highly structured routine there is no reason why you shouldn't have one. What *is* essential is to have clear strategies for indicating, politely but firmly, when you are too busy to be interrupted.

The strategies to adopt depend to some extent upon you, as what appeals to one person doesn't necessarily appeal to another. The essential thing is to be consistent in the use of these strategies; chopping and changing gives people the idea that any rules you make for the management of your time can be broken by others just where and when they feel like it.

SOME RECOMMENDED STRATEGIES

There are a number of strategies which can be helpful, and they can be used singly or in combination, whichever seems best. The most useful can be summarized as follows:

☐ Don't leave your office door open unless your job is specifically involved with encouraging people to come and talk to you. Some individuals, particularly those who are extroverted, have a habit of doing this. It enables them to watch life go by, and to feel they're part of it instead of isolated in their own world. But an open door is an invitation for people to drop in, whether they've got anything important to say to you or not. A closed door may look a little antisocial, but you can't manage time *and* be the permanent life and soul of the party.

☐ Make three signs for your door (more if you feel like it). One should say 'Available', another 'Busy', and the third 'Desperately Busy'. Change them around as necessary.

☐ Identify the colleagues who, when they call on you, are likely to overstay their welcome. Decide in advance how much time under normal circumstances you can allow them, and have a form of words to end your conversation with them when that time is up. Refer in your words to specific work and time constraints. 'I must finish this by lunch-time' is much better than 'I've got work to do', while 'X wants this by tomorrow' is much better than 'I'm working on something for X'.

☐ State that you'll continue the conversation later. If it's a colleague or a friend 'later' may mean over lunch or over coffee. Make a clear statement to this effect (which indicates you've already made up your mind) rather than issue an invitation or offer a question (which indicates the matter is open to debate). For example, 'We'll talk it over at lunch' is much better than, 'Shall we talk it over at lunch?'

☐ Make public your decision to manage time more effectively (see Chapter 4), and ensure that colleagues and friends understand some of the details of how you intend going about it. This won't stop certain of them from interrupting you at inconvenient times, but it will make it easier for you to remind them how busy you are.

☐ If you have a secretary, ask him or her to indicate to callers when you are not available, and to offer to take a message. Casual callers usually say there isn't one, and on the occasions when there actually is something for the secretary to write down, it will usually take much less time to read and deal with than it would have taken in the actual telling.

☐ Whenever possible, go to the room of a talkative colleague if there is something to be discussed, rather than invite them to come to you. This makes it much easier for you to end the conversation, especially if you remain standing. If they have to come to you, schedule the meeting for just before lunch or just before another set commitment so that things have to be kept relatively short.

☐ If the worst comes to the worst, lock your door, put your head down, place your fingers metaphorically in your ears, and get on with your work as if your very life depends upon it (as it just might; few things contribute more to stress-related illnesses than the frustrations caused by urgent work to which you're never allowed to give your undivided attention).

These strategies work well when people are actually physically present in the room with you, but they're less use when it comes to the telephone. The telephone, for all its value as a time saver when properly used, is on occasions the enemy within. It is immune to locked doors, and blind to the social signals that indicate you're busy. It butts in on you when your mind is occupied with other matters, and allows the determined conversationalist to override your every attempt to get a word in edgeways. The only advantage it has at these times is that you can pull faces to your heart's content knowing that the person on the other end, no matter how eminent and dignified, is blissfully unaware of them!

The first step in avoiding time-loss when someone rings you is to eliminate the social small talk, however pleasant in itself, which usually precedes the real reason for the call. The best way to do this is to invite them to give this reason from the word go. 'Ben, how nice to speak to you, what can I do for you?', is thus much more economical of time than, 'Ben, how nice to speak to you, how are you?'. The second step is to make plain from the outset just how much time you have available for talking: 'I'm due in a meeting in five minutes, does that give us enough time to talk?', or, 'I'm working to a deadline on something this morning, so I'm very pushed – can I call you back?'. The third step is to know how to break off the conversation at the end of your five minutes or whatever, should the other person show no sign of doing so. If they're of the compulsive-talker variety, who give you no chance to wait for a pause in their verbal onslaught, break in on them *and keep talking until you have said what you need to say*. Most compulsive talkers are used to others falling silent if both you and they are talking together, and your determination will make them pause out of sheer surprise if nothing else. Make it clear: 'Ben, I'm sorry I'm going to have to leave it there. I'm in the middle of something which I have to finish by lunchtime, and I'm already way behind. Give me a ring at the weekend if you like'.

Notice that there are three elements in this response. Firstly you make clear that you're terminating the conversation; secondly you give a reason for doing so; and thirdly you offer an invitation to talk again at a more convenient time. If after this your compulsive friend tries to carry on the conversation ('Just another quick point before you go . . .') be firm with him or her – 'I have to ring off now Ben but I look forward to hearing about it at the weekend'. Don't fall into the mistake of apologizing or of temporizing. A lot of 'Sorry Ben, but I must . . .', 'Look Ben, I have to . . .' 'Yes I see

Ben, but I . . .' only gives Ben the signal that you're not serious about ringing off. Be polite but firm. Say what you are going to do, and do it. You won't give offence. It isn't that easy to lose the friendship of a compulsive talker.

DEALING WITH CLIENTS

In theory it should be easier to deal with time-wasting clients than with time-wasting colleagues and friends, since your relationship with clients is a more official and contractual one. In practice however it's often much harder. Whatever the area of professional life in which we work, many (perhaps most) clients come to us with problems. These may be personal, domestic, or business problems, but whether they are to do with depression or with productivity, they have one thing in common. To the person who is experiencing them, they're more pressing and obvious than your own worries over time-management. The majority of clients don't deliberately set out to make life harder for the busy professional by stealing unnecessary time, but they have no real idea of what it is like to be under the pressures with which the professional has to deal. For some clients, whatever their problems in life may happen to be, time pressures are not one of them. Some clients may, in any case, be so centred upon their own difficulties that they are oblivious to the social signals that indicate you're in a hurry.

However, many of the strategies that apply when dealing with colleagues and friends also apply when dealing with clients. Firstly, if you're too busy at the moment to spend the necessary time with them, don't be afraid to say so. It's far better to postpone a talk until a more appropriate opportunity than to listen with half an ear and end up misreading the problem. Again, don't feel you have to offer a lengthy apology. Apologies in these circumstances can sound like self-justification on the one hand or guilty evasions on the other. Simply state the circumstances ('I'm just on my way to a meeting, so now wouldn't be the right time to talk') and arrange an appointment for when you know you can be free ('Let's make it Friday at 2 o'clock'). Don't make the mistake of adding words such as 'There'll be plenty of time to talk then'. The client may then feel that they will have the monopoly of your time all Friday afternoon, when in point of fact you'll probably be only marginally less busy then than you are now.

Secondly, when you do meet for a talk, make it clear at the outset how much time you have available (for example, 'We can talk until

MORE TELEPHONE DOS AND DON'TS

For all business calls, there are several further points that can help you avoid wasting time. When making a call yourself:

Know what you want to say: have clear objectives as to what the call is about.

Prepare how you are going to say it: have the questions, explanations or pieces of information you intend to convey firmly in mind before you pick up the phone; few things are more frustrating than realizing afterwards that you've left important things unsaid.

Decide how you are going to react to obstructions at the other end of the line: determine in advance how you will deal with such contingencies as anger, unavailability, uncooperative behaviour or an answering machine.

Have all necessary documentation to hand: if you may need to refer to papers, collect them together before you phone (this avoids your having to hunt for them during the call, or worse still having to ring off and phone back later).

Be prepared to make notes: have pen and paper ready.

Try to finish your business: it's unproductive to make a call in the expectation of completing a particular task only to find yourself generating yet more work for yourself.

When taking a call, be sure you:

Hear clearly the name of the other person: request they repeat it if you don't.

When necessary ask for something in writing: if the call is an invitation of some kind and you're in doubt about it, ask for the details in writing before you commit yourself; also ask for confirmation in writing of instructions or information.

Deal with the call now if you can: unless circumstances rule it out, deal with the call now rather than offer to ring back; ringing back only adds to your jobs.

a quarter to three'). This may seem a little harsh, but remember the *Pareto Time Principle* (Chapter 5). If you allow things to run their natural course, 80 per cent of what needs to be said will probably be said in 20 per cent of the time you make available. Giving up two hours for what could effectively be said in a quarter of that time often encourages people to be slow in coming to the point, and may even result in important issues being forgotten altogether. Avoid trapping yourself into the *Pareto Time Principle* by allocating a sufficient but not lavish amount of time, and then, unless it becomes clear in the course of the interview that this isn't going to be enough, keep to it.

Thirdly, during the interview gently but firmly ensure that the client doesn't wander too far from the point ('You were telling me about . . .', 'Can we go back to what you were saying about . . .?'; 'It would help if you could tell me more about . . .'). In addition, make sure you have the opportunity to ask the questions needed to give you all the information *you* require, whether these questions are to do with clarifying what the client has been telling you ('Have I got this right? I think you're saying that . . .') or with seeking additional information ('I need to know something about . . .').

Fourthly, give the client an 'early warning' when the time available is drawing to a close. Don't simply announce, 'We've got five minutes left'. Be diplomatic but firm – 'We've only got five minutes left, and I want to make sure we've covered all the main points . . .'. When the time comes to part, again be diplomatic but firm. If you're on the client's premises, don't keep saying, 'I must be off', edging uncertainly towards the door. Say instead, 'I have to go now', and get up and cross to the door. Open it *before* shaking hands or otherwise taking your leave; this allows you to withdraw immediately after leave-taking, rather than risk being drawn into a further protracted discussion.

If you're meeting with the client on your own premises, get to your feet as soon as you feel the interview is over. Maintain eye-contact with the client as you do so. Looking vaguely into the middle distance or out of the window suggests either that you're guilty about having to bring the conversation to an end, or that you've already turned your mind to other things (both of which can lead to a determined bid by the client to recapture your attention and take up more time). Don't precede the client to the door and fling it open as if dismissing a stray dog. Walk with them to the door, guiding them with a friendly hand on the arm (if you feel this appropriate). Opening the door while *you* are still talking is more polite than opening it briskly while they are in the middle of saying something. Once the door is open, make sure they know the date of their next appointment and are clear on any further action that needs to be taken, and bring things to a close.

SAYING 'NO'

With colleagues, friends and clients alike, one of the biggest problems many of us face is how to refuse the many requests we receive to do things. We hate to feel that we are disappointing people. Saying 'no' can also sometimes suggest that we can't be bothered to help out, or are insensitive to the needs of others. But it's a fact of life that we can't do everything, and a frequent complaint made to me by people in stress workshops is that they consistently find themselves taking on far more than they can reasonably (or productively) handle.

Before discussing some of the most effective (and least hurtful) ways of saying 'no', ask yourself whether, in your approach to professional life, you are primarily *task-orientated* or *people-orientated* (for some people the orientation is situation-specific; they will be task-orientated in certain circumstances and people-orientated in others). If you are the former, this means that you tend to focus attention on the job itself rather than on the people associated with it, and make your decisions accordingly, while if you are the latter it's the other way around. Obviously, in many ways it is easier for those who are task-orientated to say 'no', than for those who are people-orientated, since, when requested to do something, the former tend to ask themselves, 'Am I able to do this?' (or 'Do I want to do it?' or, 'Can I find time to do it?') while the latter are more likely to enquire, 'Can I disappoint this person?'

It would be wrong to say whether it is better to be task-oriented or people-oriented. Ideally, we should be a combination of both. But if you're people-oriented and want to be more effective at saying 'no', prompt yourself to think more carefully about the *task* involved each time you're asked to take on something. Is it realistic to expect yourself to do it, and to do it well? Can you fit it in around your other commitments? If the dates involved are far in the future, don't assume your life is going to be any less crowded then than it is now. Also, take steps to clarify the task. What exactly will it involve? How much time will it take up? If you find it's too much for you once you embark upon it, will you be able to withdraw without causing too many problems? If the answers to these questions indicate you'd be unwise to take it on, then it is neither in the interests of the people who are asking you nor in your own interests to say yes to it.

Even individuals who are primarily task-oriented are not immune to problems over saying 'no' however, though for them these problems take a rather different form. Here the difficulty sometimes faced is that they have to learn to be able to say 'no' to tasks they *enjoy* doing as well as those they don't. This can be difficult. A task may sound so attractive that there's a big temptation to agree to it, and to tell yourself that the business of actually fitting it in can be worried about later. But worrying about it later isn't likely to be any easier than worrying about it now. No matter how enticing the task, the only sensible thing is to work out whether taking it on is feasible or not *before* agreeing to it. Once agreement is given, it's far worse for everyone if you have to pull out later.

Other factors that sometimes make things difficult are the need to be wanted or liked, and the boost to the ego that comes from being in great demand. These are matters that need to be recognized and explored at a personal level, but it may be helpful to point out that that if we take on too much and end up failing to do anything to the best of our ability, this will not increase our chances of being liked or improve our ego-esteem. Far better for everyone concerned if we work within sensible limits, and ensure that some of our energy goes into quality as well as quantity.

SOME GUIDELINES FOR SAYING 'NO'

For people-orientated and task-orientated individuals alike, here are some useful guidelines for saying 'no':

☐ Categorize and assign priorities to the tasks you're likely to be asked to do. In an extra-busy phase of your life you may decide that you can only take on the tasks that fall into the top categories; when things are less hectic, you may be able to consider lower categories as well.

☐ Decide how far ahead you want to commit yourself. Agreeing to a one-off task 12 months hence may seem fine now, but nearer the date you may discover you have been invited to be away around the time concerned, or to take on something more worthwhile or more extensive that is going to clash with it. Other people not unnaturally think it's easier to book a busy person if they do it well in advance, but often the reverse is true. So if your commitments ahead are uncertain, only agree to something that's in the foreseeable future.

□ Make sure you're not caught unprepared. It's often harder to say 'no' if someone springs a request on you unexpectedly. Be ready for the fact that under certain circumstances and in certain situations you're almost bound to be asked to take on a commitment. Have a form of words ready which allows you to decline firmly but politely. If in doubt, ask for time to think it over. It's unfair to expect you always to be able to give an immediate response.

□ Don't sound too apologetic. You don't gain respect by profuse and detailed expressions of regret. Say whatever has to be said briefly and clearly, and stick to it. If people get the idea that you can be made to change your mind, they'll keep coming back to you until they've got you to agree.

□ Don't feel guilty about saying 'no'. Provided you have a good reason, you have every right to decline a request. If you worry yourself with feelings of guilt after saying 'no' you'll be much more likely to succumb to the next request that comes your way, however low in priority.

FORMS OF WORDS
The best rule is that the form of words you use to say 'no' should *express regret, be definite, be polite,* and *contain a reason.* This last isn't essential of course, but giving a reason does help the other person to see that you're not turning down their request because you simply can't be bothered with it. It can also avoid your being approached again. To make sure of this, give a reason that is accurate. If you say you're too busy just at the moment, rather than making it clear you're not the right person for the job, then in all probability you'll be confronted with a follow-up request to give a time when things are likely to be easier for you, and it will become increasingly hard to refuse.

Examples of appropriate forms of words are: 'I'm sorry but that isn't my field', 'For the foreseeable future I can't consider taking on any more engagements, I'm afraid', 'Sorry, but in fairness to my family I'm cutting down on my commitments'. Notice that these examples avoid such forms of words as: 'I'm not up to the job/I haven't the experience for the job' (which invites people to flatter you by telling you that you are/you have), 'You need someone who knows about . . .' (which invites them to say no, they don't, they need someone like you) or 'I'd like to do it but . . .' (which invites them to persuade you that since you'd like to do it, in kindness to yourself you should accept).

It's also right to point out to people that if you take on more work you won't be able to do your existing tasks properly, or that you're already under too much pressure for the good of your health, or that you've been saying 'no' to similar requests from other people and in fairness to them you can't make an exception now. But however you put it, suit your tone of voice to your words. Even the most clear-cut of refusals sounds unconvincing if delivered in a hesitant (or guilty) manner.

SAYING 'NO' TO YOUR SUPERIORS

Saying 'no' to superiors is a rather different exercise from saying 'no' to colleagues, friends, and clients, firstly because what they're asking you to do may seem like part of your job, secondly because you may be afraid of appearing work-shy, and thirdly because you know that as a last resort they can turn round and tell you that you have to do it anyway.

The only reasons likely to be acceptable when saying 'no' to superiors are that if you take on the new task existing work will suffer, or that the new task doesn't lie within your area of competence. Both these reasons sound more convincing if you support them with specific instances. For example, you may be able to show that the new task would need to be carried out at a time that clearly clashes with an important existing commitment. Or you may be able to list skills that it requires and which it is acknowledged you don't have. Be accurate, brief and to the point in giving these reasons. It's disastrous if your boss succeeds in disproving your arguments on factual grounds alone, and gives the clear impression that he or she suspects you of trumping up the feeblest of excuses – or of being so incompetent that you haven't been able to go into matters properly.

It can be helpful to back up these reasons by listing the extra tasks you have taken on lately, or by referring to new tasks that are known to await you in the near future. Don't fire off too many excuses though. This is an invitation to the boss to pick on the weakest of them, show it doesn't hold water, and then dismiss your argument without even referring to the stronger reasons (and with the news to boot that the new task is yours anyway and you'd better make a success of it).

A further useful strategy is to come up with a clear suggestion as to how the new task can be handled without placing the full load on your shoulders. If you're Machiavellian enough to allow the boss to think this is his or her idea, so much the better. If you're even more Machiavellian, you may be able to turn the new task into an opportunity to off-load some existing chores you dislike. By accepting the new task with good grace and then suggesting you relinquish these latter 'in order to give it the time and attention it deserves' you may find your boss agreeing with you before he or she quite realizes what is happening. But this is a matter for your own judgement!

TIME LOST WORRYING ABOUT CRITICISMS FROM OTHERS

Time lost worrying about anything, if there is clearly nothing we can do to put it right, is time badly spent. (And we're all aware of what a time-thief worrying can be – note how we say 'I can't waste time worrying about that now', 'I've no time to worry on that score', and so on.) The simple rule is that if there *is* something to be done, do it now. If not, put the matter out of your mind (easier said than done, but worth working on). This applies particularly when it comes to worrying about the behaviour of other people towards us, in particular the clashes of personality that are almost inevitable from time to time with colleagues or with clients, or about the criticisms that are made of us, or about the motives that may (or may not) underlie the words or actions of others in relation to us.

Most people know from bitter experience how easy it is for us to lose an afternoon's work while we churn over unproductively in our minds some barbed remark that was made to us earlier in the day. We go over and over the remark and the incident that led to it, each time feeling more aggrieved about it, and only when the mind becomes thoroughly weary of it are we eventually able to turn to something else. When incidents like this happen, *think about them only long enough to learn from them*. How for example can the incident be avoided in the future? How might you have handled it more effectively? Is there any follow-up needed (not in order to get your own back, but to clear up any important misunderstandings)?

Once this learning has taken place, drop the incident from your mind.

How is this dropping done? The better your powers of concentration, the easier it is. The concentrated mind can turn from one thing to another, placing attention always on what is being done *now*. So by turning back to work and placing full attention there, the unpleasant incident of a few moments ago is quickly forgotten. If you find concentration difficult, then there is a simple exercise that can help (see page 109). Concentration is in fact an invaluable aid in all areas of time-management, as it prevents the mind from constantly being distracted by all the extraneous things that may be clamouring for your attention, and it is well worth devoting regular time to these exercises.

In addition to concentration, it's as well to reflect that if someone intended to upset you by his or her remarks, then if you dwell on them unnecessarily he or she has succeeded in their aim. Reflect also on your self-image. One reason why criticism or slighting remarks can wound us is that they threaten this self-image. If people think badly of us or of our work, it suggests to us that we may not be the person we thought we were (or the person we hope to be). Self-image can be a fragile thing. Underneath our confident exterior we're all inclined to doubt our worth at times. We've been brought up to doubt it. Throughout the formative years of childhood most of us were frequently told by parents and/or teachers that we were falling short of their required standards. Little wonder that even in adult life we're uncertain about ourselves. If criticism wounds you unduly, measure it against a realistic self-image. Try to keep emotions out of the picture. If the criticism is justified (and even ill-meant criticism can often be helpful when viewed objectively) learn from it. If not, dismiss it. And resolve in future to try and be more secure about yourself, to recognize more clearly your strengths, and not to be so easily deflected from this realization by the insensitive words of others.

Finally, resolve not to speculate unnecessarily about the motives that may or may not underlie some of the actions or words of others towards you. There are occasions when it is important to try and identify these motives, but they can be few and far between. For the most part, the time lost speculating about what other people meant by this or that action or this or that remark is time wasted. Other people must take responsibility for their own approach to life; your task is to do the best you can with the abilities and qualities – and time – given to you.

CONCENTRATION

All of us admire people with powers of intense concentration – people who can keep their minds focused upon one particular task (interesting or dull) instead of becoming distracted by their own thoughts or by stimuli from outside. There's a tendency to assume that they just happen to be born that way, unlike most of the rest of us. In fact, although people may differ in their potential to develop concentration, there is no reason at all why the vast majority of us should be unable to develop all the powers we need. Concentration is one of those skills that transfers across tasks – if we can concentrate well on one thing then potentially we can concentrate well on other things too.

The three essentials in developing concentration are *motivation*, *self-discipline*, and *practice*. The problem with most of us is that we've got into the habit over the years of allowing our minds to wander. This is hardly surprising, as we have so many things to think about. But much of our thinking is in fact very wasteful, and doesn't get us anywhere. It goes over and over the same ground, throwing up a ragbag of memories, hopes, anxieties, expectations, and we rummage through it for much of our waking lives. Try and stop thinking for just one minute. The chances are you can't do it (and remember that thinking 'I'm not thinking' is still a thought!).

Provided you start with sufficient motivation and apply yourself with reasonable self-discipline, you can tame your mind to stay concentrated upon what *you* want it to think about, and even to have periods when thoughts barely rise at all (an invaluable aid to relaxation). But practice is essential, as is perseverance, if only for a few minutes a day.

The secret of this practice is to find a single stimulus and to concentrate upon that. Each time the mind wanders off, bring it gently back. Don't become impatient with yourself, and above all don't give up.

A good stimulus with which to work is your breathing. Sit upright in a chair with a straight back, put your feet flat on the floor and allow your hands, with fingers interlaced, to rest palms upwards on your lap. The eyes can be open or closed (at first it's best to work with them closed, but as your concentration develops over the weeks, practise with them open sometimes). Breath slowly and from the diaphragm, as low down as possible. Now concentrate upon the gentle rise and fall of the abdomen. Count '1' on the first out-breath, '2' on the next and so on up to 10, then go back and start again at '1'. Should you lose track of your counting, go back to '1' each time. That's all, and in theory very simple. If your concentration seems poor, don't be discouraged. This just shows how much you need to practise.

You'll find this technique excellent in mustering your concentration before a particular task, in helping release your creativity, and in calming and in refreshing you. It's the basic technique not just of concentration-training but also for meditation (see Fontana, 1991). Some days it will work well, on others your mind will just refuse to stop chattering. Again, don't be discouraged. Note what you are learning about your mind in its different moods. And keep practising – for five minutes a day at first, then gradually for longer periods.

ORGANIZATIONAL ISSUES

In addition to the issues associated specifically with colleagues and clients, time can be lost as a result of the organizational structures within which we have to work. Some of these structures may lie outside our control, but it is important to identify where these structures go wrong so that whenever change is possible steps can be taken to bring it about.

Every organization is characterized by the way in which it divides its work into different tasks, and by the way in which it co-ordinates these tasks (Payne, 1984). Both these characteristics can be responsible for organizational time loss. The distribution of tasks may be uneven or unfair, with great emphasis being placed upon unimportant tasks, while important ones are virtually ignored. High status tasks may be jealously guarded by those incompetent at carrying them out, while low status tasks may be given to the more able. The organization as a whole may take on, or perhaps be forced to take on, work for which it isn't properly equipped, while individuals may lack the necessary training to carry out assigned tasks effectively and efficiently.

The co-ordination of tasks may be affected by poor communication between people, and the chain of command may be obscure or nonexistent. Some tasks may actively interfere with the carrying out or delegation of others, while some tasks may be performed in the wrong order, or may duplicate or overlap with each other. There may be no avenues through which individuals can make known their suggestions for improved effectiveness and/or efficiency. Problems of this kind, together with specific task-related difficulties, can leave individuals unable to participate in the processes which lead to organizational change and improvement, resulting in great time-loss, frustration and professional stress (Margolis *et al*. 1974).

The essential first step in effecting organizational change in the area of time-management is to draw attention to the existence of the problem. In most cases it is best to do this formally. Informal discussions with colleagues can be of help, but in my own experience they all too often become a substitute for action. People complain together over lunch or coffee, get their frustrations off their chests, and then do nothing further. Raising the matter formally draws proper attention to its existence, and places an onus upon the organization either to recognize the need and the possibilities for change, or to put on record the reasons why it is inappropriate or impossible.

There are a number of ways in which formal attention can be drawn to the problem, although the most usual is to put it on the agenda of a routine meeting or to request that a special meeting be convened. Whatever the procedure, the second step in effecting organizational change is to spell out the issues in a discussion paper which should be circulated to all concerned. The paper should be kept brief and to the point; there is no virtue in a paper on good time-management which wastes the reader's time in rambling irrelevancies and repetitions. Conduct some observational research beforehand so that the paper:

• identifies where time is currently being lost, both in terms of tasks and in terms of the co-ordination between tasks;

• identifies what can be done to improve matters;

• advances specific recommendations for effecting this improvement.

Where appropriate, a working party can be formed to implement these recommendations, to monitor future progress and to report back regularly. But irrespective of whether a working party is involved or not, the third step in organizational change is to make sure that there is adequate follow-up. Organizations can all too easily become set in their ways, and only an ongoing programme of appraisal, modification and reform is likely to prevent this happening.

If there is likely to be major resistance on the part of some colleagues to your initiative in trying to effect appropriate organizational change, it is good policy to try and quantify the working hours currently lost through poor time-management, and, where appropriate, to cost this time in hard financial terms. Finally, it hardly needs saying that if you do take this initiative and draw attention to the poor time-management strategies operating within the organization, you will inevitably draw attention to your own personal time-management behaviours. Thus you will have a further incentive to make sure that these behaviours are as effective and efficient as possible!

CONCLUSION

I said at the end of Chapter 5 that managing time has a lot to do with managing life, and I want to end by re-emphasizing this. It is difficult to manage time if we see the process as simply a set of techniques which we hope to graft onto an unchanged life-style. I began this book by making reference to the fact that time is finite capital and not renewable income. Time is ever hurrying by, the present moment ever receding into the irrecoverable past. 'Where *does* the time go?' we find ourselves constantly asking, and almost before we know it this question will change to 'Where *did* the time go?'. Between my opening references to time as capital and these closing sentences, I've written this book. Between your encounter with these opening references and with these closing sentences you've read it. Where has the time for both of us gone? Have we used it to good effect? The one sure thing about it is that it will never return to either of us.

REFERENCES

Baddeley, A. (1983) *Your Memory: A User's Guide.* Harmondsworth: Penguin Books.

Brown, M. (1979) *Memory Matters.* New York: Sphere Books.

Christie, B. (1984) Office systems. In C.L. Cooper and P. Makin (Eds) *Psychology for Managers.* Leicester: BPS Books (The British Psychological Society) and Macmillan. (Out of print, available from libraries.)

Christie, B. and Kingan, S. (1977) Electronic alternatives to the business meeting: managers' choices. *Journal of Occupational Psychology 50,* 265–273.

Drucker, P. (1982) *The Effective Executive.* London: Heinemann.

Erikson, E. (1968) *Identity: Youth and Crisis.* New York: Norton.

Fontana, D. (1988) *Psychology for Teachers.* Leicester: BPS Books (The British Psychological Society) and Macmillan.

Fontana, D. (1990) *Social Skills at Work.* Leicester: BPS Books (The British Psychological Society) and Routledge.

Fontana, D. (1991) *The Elements of Meditation.* Shaftesbury: Element Books.

Halberg, F. (1960) The 24-hour scale: a time dimension of adaptive functional organization. *Perspectives in Biology and Medicine 3,* 491–498.

Horowitz, F.D. (1987) *Exploring Developmental Theories: Towards a Structural/Behavioural Model of Development.* Hillsdale, N.J.: Erlbaum.

Klatzky, R.L. (1980) *Human Memory: Structure and Processes.* San Francisco: Freeman.

Margolis, B.L., Kroes, W.H. and Quinn, R.P. (1974) Job stress: an unlisted occupational hazard. *Journal of Occupational Medicine 16,* 654–661.

Mintzberg, H. (1973) *The Nature of Managerial Work.* New York: Harper and Row.

Mintzberg, H. (1979) *The Structure of Organizations.* Englewood Cliffs N.J.: Prentice Hall.

Nelson-Jones, R. (1986) *Human Relationship Skills: Training and Self-Help.* London: Cassell.

Payne, R. (1984) Organizational behaviour. In C.L. Cooper and P. Makin (Eds) *Psychology for Managers.* Leicester: BPS Books (The British Psychological Society) and Macmillan. (Out of print, available from libraries.)

Pearn, M. and Kandola, R. (1988) *Job Analysis: A Practical Guide for Managers.* London: Institute of Personnel Management.

Pearson, L. and Tweddle, D. (1984) The formulation and use of educational objectives. In D. Fontana (Ed.) *Behaviourism and Learning Theory in Education.* Edinburgh: Scottish Academic Press.

Reynolds, H. and Tramel, M.E. (1985) *Executive Time Management.* London: Gower Press.

Seiwert, L. (1991) *Time is Money.* London: Kogan Page.

Skinner, B.F. (1972) *Cumulative Record: A Selection of Papers.* New York: Appleton Century-Crofts, 3rd edn.

Weiner, B. (1979) A theory of motivation for some classroom experience. *Journal of Educational Psychology, 71,* 3–25.

FURTHER READING

Blanchard, K. and Johnson, S. (1984) *The One Minute Manager*. London: Fontana.

Bliss, E.C. (1985) *Getting Things Done: The ABCs of Time Management*. New York: Futura.

Ferner, J.D. (1980) *Successful Time Management*. New York: Wiley.

Holland, G. (1984) *Running a Business Meeting*. New York: Dell.

Januz, L.R. and Jones, S.K. (1981) *Time-Management for Executives*. New York: Scribner.

Knaus, W.J. (1979) *Do It Now: Stop Procrastinating*. New York: Prentice Hall.

Love, S.F. (1978) *Mastery and Management of Time*. New York: Prentice Hall.

Noon, J. (1983) *Time for Success*. London: Thompson.

Taylor, H.L. (1984) *Delegate: The Key to Successful Management*. New York: General Publishing.

Index